Margin of Safety

MARGIN OF SAFETY

Risk-Averse Value Investing Strategies for the Thoughtful Investor

Seth A. Klarman

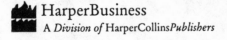 HarperBusiness
A *Division of* HarperCollins*Publishers*

Library of Congress Cataloging-in Publication Data

Klarman, Seth A. 1957—
    Margin of Safety: risk-averse value investing strategies for the thoughtful investor/Seth A. Klarman.
        p. cm.
    Includes bibliographical references and index.
    1. Investment.   2. Stocks.   3. Junk bonds.   I. Title.
    HG4521.K566   1991   91–32049
    332.6'78—dc20   CIP
ISBN:0–88730–510–5

Printed in the United States of America

    92 93 94 SWD/HC 9 8 7 6 5 4 3 2

To my girls
and
Dedicated to the memory of
Max L. Heine,
my mentor and
my friend

Contents

Acknowledgments

While always interested in the workings of Wall Street, I was extremely fortunate in my first real job to have the opportunity to work alongside Michael Price and the late Max L. Heine at Mutual Shares Corporation (now Mutual Series Fund, Inc.). My uncle Paul Friedman always encouraged my interest in investing and helped me land that job. I look back on my experience at Mutual Shares very fondly. My learning in the two years working with Max and Mike probably eclipsed what I learned in the subsequent two years at Harvard Business School. It is to Max's memory that I dedicate this book.

After earning my MBA at Harvard, I was faced with several exciting career choices. The unconventional offer to join a start-up investment-management firm in Cambridge, Massachusetts, presented the opportunity to begin building an investment track record early in my career. And so it was that I joined Bill Poorvu, Isaac Auerbach, Jordan Baruch, Howard Stevenson, and Jo-An Bosworth in forming the Baupost Group. Each of my colleagues—Howard in particular—went out on a long, thin limb to bet on me and my abilities, not only to manage their own money but also that of their families and close friends, which was perhaps the greater act of faith. It has been my great privilege to be associated with such knowledgeable, energetic, warm, and caring people. Together we have built something to be proud of.

It has also been a privilege to work alongside Paul O'Leary, David Abrams, and now Tom Knott, my brilliant and dedicated investment team and in-house doubles game. I am grateful to each of them for his many insights and observations, a number of which appear in one form or another in this work.

I am also fortunate to have some of the finest clients a professional investor could have. A number of them encouraged me in this endeavor. While I shall respect their privacy by not naming them, their patience, interest, and support have been key elements in our investment success.

My nine years at Baupost have brought me into contact with many of the finest people in the investment business, on both the buy side and the sell side. I am grateful to each of them for teaching me so much about this business and for putting up with me when I was having a bad day. Though they are too numerous to thank individually, I owe each of them a great deal.

I do wish to thank the people who have been especially helpful with this project. My colleagues at Baupost—Howard, David, Paul, and Tom—each reviewed the manuscript as it neared completion as did four special friends, Lou Lowenstein, David Darst, Henry Emerson, and Bret Fromson. A number of other friends made very helpful suggestions at earlier stages of this project. Jess Ravich, in particular, offered many valuable insights into the junk-bond and bankruptcy sections. Finally, Jim Grant, perhaps without realizing it, inspired me to take on this challenge. I thank each of them for their help, and far more important, I will always cherish their friendship.

My wife, Beth Klarman, offered the fresh perspective of a non-financial-professional as she devotedly read every chapter and made numerous helpful recommendations. She also made every accommodation to help free up time for me to devote to this project and urged me to press on to completion the many times when progress was slow. I thank her for being a great wife and mother and my best friend.

My father, Herb Klarman, was perhaps the most careful reader of multiple drafts of this manuscript. He is a true craftsman of the art of writing, and his comments are literally incorporated on every page of this book. I thank him for his tremendous assistance. I also want to thank my mother, Muriel Klarman, for teaching me to ask questions and encouraging me to discover the answers.

Finally I must acknowledge the extraordinary efforts of Mark Greenberg, my editor at HarperBusiness, and Mitch Tuchman, my developmental editor, in improving this manuscript in so many ways. I thank them both for their help in seeing this project to fruition. I also owe thanks to Martha Jewett, who made helpful comments on an early draft, and special thanks to Virginia Smith, who proposed this project out of the blue.

Jacqui Fiorenza, Mike Hammond, and Susie Spero were of enormous assistance with the typing and retyping of this manuscript. Kathryn Potts made numerous editorial suggestions and helped to prepare the glossary. Carolyn Beckedorff provided research assistance as needed.

As with any work such as this, full responsibility for errors must be borne by the author. I hope those that remain are minor and few in number.

Introduction

Investors adopt many different approaches that offer little or no real prospect of long-term success and considerable chance of substantial economic loss. Many are not coherent investment programs at all but instead resemble speculation or outright gambling. Investors are frequently lured by the prospect of quick and easy gain and fall victim to the many fads of Wall Street. My goals in writing this book are twofold. In the first section I identify many of the pitfalls that face investors. By highlighting where so many go wrong, I hope to help investors learn to avoid these losing strategies.

For the remainder of the book I recommend one particular path for investors to follow—a value-investment philosophy. Value investing, the strategy of investing in securities trading at an appreciable discount from underlying value, has a long history of delivering excellent investment results with very limited downside risk. This book explains the philosophy of value investing and, perhaps more importantly, the logic behind it in an attempt to demonstrate why it succeeds while other approaches fail.

I have chosen to begin this book, not with a discussion of what value investors do right, but with an assessment of where other investors go wrong, for many more investors lose their way along the road to investment success than reach their destination. It is easy to stray but a continuous effort to remain disciplined. Avoiding where others go wrong is an important step in achieving investment success. In fact, it almost ensures it.

You may be wondering, as several of my friends have, why I would write a book that could encourage more people to become value investors. Don't I run the risk of encouraging increased competition, thereby reducing my own investment returns? Perhaps, but I do not believe this will happen. For one thing, value investing is not being discussed here for the first time. While I have tried to build the case for it somewhat differently from my predecessors and while my precise philosophy may vary from that of other value investors, a number of these views have been expressed before, notably by Benjamin Graham and David Dodd, who more than fifty years ago wrote *Security Analysis*, regarded by many as the bible of value investing. That single work has illuminated the way for generations of value investors. More recently Graham wrote *The Intelligent Investor*, a less academic description of the value-investment process. Warren Buffett, the chairman of Berkshire Hathaway, Inc., and a student of Graham, is regarded as today's most successful value investor. He has written countless articles and shareholder and partnership letters that together articulate his value-investment philosophy coherently and brilliantly. Investors who have failed to heed such wise counsel are unlikely to listen to me.

The truth is, I am pained by the disastrous investment results experienced by great numbers of unsophisticated or undisciplined investors. If I can persuade just a few of them to avoid dangerous investment strategies and adopt sound ones that are designed to preserve and maintain their hard-earned capital, I will be satisfied. If I should have a wider influence on investor behavior, then I would gladly pay the price of a modest diminution in my own investment returns.

In any event this book alone will not turn anyone into a successful value investor. Value investing requires a great deal of hard work, unusually strict discipline, and a long-term investment horizon. Few are willing and able to devote sufficient time and effort to become value investors, and only a fraction of those have the proper mind-set to succeed.

This book most certainly does not provide a surefire formula for investment success. There is, of course, no such formula. Rather this book is a blueprint that, if carefully followed, offers a good possibility of investment success with limited risk. I believe this is as much as investors can reasonably hope for.

Ideally this will be considered, not a book about investing, but a book about thinking about investing. Like most eighth-grade algebra students, some investors memorize a few formulas or rules and superficially appear competent but do not really understand what they are doing. To achieve long-term success over many financial market and economic cycles, observing a few rules is not enough. Too many things change too quickly in the investment world for that approach to succeed. It is necessary instead to understand the rationale behind the rules in order to appreciate why they work when they do and don't when they don't. I could simply assert that value investing works, but I hope to show you *why* it works and why most other approaches do not.

If interplanetary visitors landed on Earth and examined the workings of our financial markets and the behavior of financial-market participants, they would no doubt question the intelligence of the planet's inhabitants. Wall Street, the financial marketplace where capital is allocated worldwide, is in many ways just a gigantic casino. The recipient of up-front fees on every transaction, Wall Street clearly is more concerned with the volume of activity than its economic utility. Pension and endowment funds responsible for the security and enhancement of long-term retirement, educational, and philanthropic resources employ investment managers who frenetically trade long-term securities on a very short-term basis, each trying to outguess and consequently outperform others doing the same thing. In addition, hundreds of billions of dollars are invested in virtual or complete ignorance of underlying business fundamentals, often using indexing strategies designed to avoid significant underperformance at the cost of assured mediocrity.

Individual and institutional investors alike frequently demonstrate an inability to make long-term investment decisions based on business fundamentals. There are a number of reasons for this: among them the performance pressures faced by institutional investors, the compensation structure of Wall Street, and the frenzied atmosphere of the financial markets. As a result, investors, particularly institutional investors, become enmeshed in a short-term relative-performance derby, whereby temporary price fluctuations become the dominant focus. Relative-performance-oriented investors, already focused on short-term returns, frequently are attracted to the latest market fads as a source of superior relative performance. The temptation of making a fast buck is great, and many investors find it difficult to fight the crowd.

Investors are sometimes their own worst enemies. When prices are generally rising, for example, greed leads investors to speculate, to make substantial, high-risk bets based upon optimistic predictions, and to focus on return while ignoring risk. At the other end of the emotional spectrum, when prices are generally falling, fear of loss causes investors to focus solely on the possibility of continued price declines to the exclusion of investment fundamentals. Regardless of the market environment, many investors seek a formula for success. The unfortunate reality is that investment success cannot be captured in a mathematical equation or a computer program.

The first section of this book, chapters 1 through 4, examines some of the places where investors stumble. Chapter 1 explores the differences between investing and speculation and between successful and unsuccessful investors, examining in particular the role of market price in investor behavior. Chapter 2 looks at the way Wall Street, with its short-term orientation, conflicts of interest, and upward bias, maximizes its own best interests, which are not necessarily also those of investors. Chapter 3 examines the behavior of institutional investors, who have come to dominate today's financial markets.

Chapter 4 uses the case study of junk bonds to illustrate

many of the pitfalls highlighted in the first three chapters. The rapid growth of the market for newly issued junk bonds was only made possible by the complicity of investors who suspended disbelief. Junk-bond buyers greedily accepted promises of a free lunch and willingly adopted new and unproven methods of analysis. Neither Wall Street nor the institutional investment community objected vocally to the widespread proliferation of these flawed instruments.

Investors must recognize that the junk-bond mania was not a once-in-a-millennium madness but instead part of the historical ebb and flow of investor sentiment between greed and fear. The important point is not merely that junk bonds were flawed (although they certainly were) but that investors must learn from this very avoidable debacle to escape the next enticing market fad that will inevitably come along.

A second important reason to examine the behavior of other investors and speculators is that their actions often inadvertently result in the creation of opportunities for value investors. Institutional investors, for example, frequently act as lumbering behemoths, trampling some securities to large discounts from underlying value even as they ignore or constrain themselves from buying others. Those they decide to purchase they buy with gusto; many of these favorites become significantly overvalued, creating selling (and perhaps short-selling) opportunities. Herds of individual investors acting in tandem can similarly bid up the prices of some securities to crazy levels, even as others are ignored or unceremoniously dumped. Abetted by Wall Street brokers and investment bankers, many individual as well as institutional investors either ignore or deliberately disregard underlying business value, instead regarding stocks solely as pieces of paper to be traded back and forth.

The disregard for investment fundamentals sometimes affects the entire stock market. Consider, for example, the enormous surge in share prices between January and August of 1987 and the ensuing market crash in October of that year. In the words of William Ruane and Richard Cunniff, chairman and president of the Sequoia Fund, Inc., "Disregarding for the moment whether the prevailing level of stock prices on January 1, 1987 was logical, we are certain that the *value* of American industry in the aggregate had not increased by 44% as of August 25. Similarly, it is highly unlikely that the *value* of American industry declined by 23% on a single day, October 19."[1]

Ultimately investors must choose sides. One side—the wrong choice—is a seemingly effortless path that offers the comfort of consensus. This course involves succumbing to the forces that guide most market participants, emotional responses dictated by greed and fear and a short-term orientation emanating from the relative-performance derby. Investors following this road increasingly think of stocks like sowbellies, as commodities to be bought and sold. This ultimately requires investors to spend their time guessing what other market participants may do and then trying to do it first. The problem is that the exciting possibility of high near-term returns from playing the stocks-as-pieces-of-paper-that-you-trade game blinds investors to its foolishness.

The correct choice for investors is obvious but requires a level of commitment most are unwilling to make. This choice is known as fundamental analysis, whereby stocks are regarded as fractional ownership of the underlying businesses that they represent. One form of fundamental analysis—and the strategy that I recommend—is an investment approach known as value investing.

There is nothing esoteric about value investing. It is simply the process of determining the value underlying a security and then buying it at a considerable discount from that value. It is really that simple. The greatest challenge is maintaining the requisite patience and discipline to buy only when prices are attractive and to sell when they are not, avoiding the short-term performance frenzy that engulfs most market participants.

The focus of most investors differs from that of value investors. Most investors are primarily oriented toward return, how much they can make, and pay little attention to risk, how much they can lose. Institutional investors, in particular, are usually evaluated—and therefore measure themselves—on the basis of relative performance compared to the market as a whole, to a relevant market sector, or to their peers.

Value investors, by contrast, have as a primary goal the preservation of their capital. It follows that value investors seek a margin of safety, allowing room for imprecision, bad luck, or analytical error in order to avoid sizable losses over time. A margin of safety is necessary because valuation is an imprecise art, the future is unpredictable, and investors are human and do make mistakes. It is adherence to the concept of a margin of safety that best distinguishes value investors from all others, who are not as concerned about loss.

If investors could predict the future direction of the market, they would certainly not choose to be value investors all the time. Indeed, when securities prices are steadily increasing, a value approach is usually a handicap; out-of-favor securities tend to rise less than the public's favorites. When the market becomes fully valued on its way to being overvalued, value investors again fare poorly because they sell too soon.

The most beneficial time to be a value investor is when the market is falling. This is when downside risk matters and when investors who worried only about what could go right suffer the consequences of undue optimism. Value investors invest with a margin of safety that protects them from large losses in declining markets.

Those who can predict the future should participate fully, indeed on margin using borrowed money, when the market is about to rise and get out of the market before it declines. Unfortunately, many more investors claim the ability to foresee the market's direction than actually possess that ability. (I myself have not met a single one.) Those of us who know that we cannot accurately forecast security prices are well advised to consider value investing, a safe and successful strategy in all investment environments.

The second section of this book, chapters 5 through 8, explores the philosophy and substance of value investing. Chapter 5 examines why most investors are risk averse and discusses the investment implications of this attitude. Chapter 6 describes the philosophy of value investing and the meaning and importance of a margin of safety. Chapter 7 considers three important underpinnings to value investing: a bottom-up approach to investment selection, an absolute-performance orientation, and analytical emphasis on risk as well as return. Chapter 8 demonstrates the principal methods of securities valuation used by value investors.

The third section of this book, chapters 9 through 14, describes the value-investment process, the implementation of a value-investment philosophy. Chapter 9 explores the research and analytical process, where value investors get their ideas and how they evaluate them. Chapter 10 illustrates a number of different value-investment opportunities ranging from corporate liquidations to spinoffs and risk arbitrage. Chapters 11 and 12 examine two specialized value-investment niches: thrift conversions and financially distressed and bankrupt securities, respectively. Chapter 13 highlights the importance of good portfolio management and trading strategies. Finally, Chapter 14 provides some insight into the possible selection of an investment professional to manage your money.

The value discipline seems simple enough but is apparently a difficult one for most investors to grasp or adhere to. As Buffett has often observed, value investing is not a concept that can be learned and applied gradually over time. It is either absorbed and adopted at once, or it is never truly learned.

I was fortunate to learn value investing at the inception of my investment career from two of its most successful practitioners: Michael Price and the late Max L. Heine of Mutual Shares Corporation. While I had been fascinated by the stock market since childhood and frequently dabbled in the market as a teenager (with modest success), working with Max and Mike was like being let in on an incredibly valuable secret. How naive all of my previous investing suddenly seemed compared with the simple but incontrovertible logic of value investing. Indeed, once you adopt a value-investment strategy, any other investment behavior starts to seem like gambling.

Throughout this book I criticize certain aspects of the investment business as currently practiced. Many of these criticisms of the industry appear as generalizations and refer more to the pressures brought about by the structure of the investment business than the failings of the individuals within it.

I also give numerous examples of specific investments throughout this book. Many of them were made over the past nine years by my firm for the benefit of our clients and indeed proved quite profitable. The fact that we made money on them is not the point, however. My goal in including them is to demonstrate the variety of value-investment opportunities that have arisen and become known to me during the past decade; an equally long and rich list of examples failed to make it into the final manuscript.

I find value investing to be a stimulating, intellectually challenging, ever changing, and financially rewarding discipline. I hope you invest the time to understand why I find it so in the pages that follow.

Notes

1. Sequoia Fund, Inc., third quarter report for 1987.

I
WHERE MOST INVESTORS STUMBLE

1

Speculators and Unsuccessful Investors

Investing Versus Speculation

Mark Twain said that there are two times in a man's life when he should not speculate: when he can't afford it and when he can. Because this is so, understanding the difference between investment and speculation is the first step in achieving investment success.

To investors stocks represent fractional ownership of underlying businesses and bonds are loans to those businesses. Investors make buy and sell decisions on the basis of the current prices of securities compared with the perceived values of those securities. They transact when they think they know something that others don't know, don't care about, or prefer to ignore. They buy securities that appear to offer attractive return for the risk incurred and sell when the return no longer justifies the risk.

Investors believe that over the long run security prices tend to reflect fundamental developments involving the underlying businesses. Investors in a stock thus expect to profit in at least one of three possible ways: from free cash flow generated by the underlying business, which eventually will be reflected in a higher share price or distributed as dividends; from an increase in the multiple that investors are willing to pay for the underlying business as reflected in a higher share price; or by a narrowing of the gap between share price and underlying business value.

Speculators, by contrast, buy and sell securities based on whether they believe those securities will next rise or fall in price. Their judgment regarding future price movements is based, not on fundamentals, but on a prediction of the behavior of others. They regard securities as pieces of paper to be swapped back and forth and are generally ignorant of or indifferent to investment fundamentals. They buy securities because they "act" well and sell when they don't. Indeed, even if it were certain that the world would end tomorrow, it is likely that some speculators would continue to trade securities based on what they thought the market would do today.

Speculators are obsessed with predicting—guessing—the direction of stock prices. Every morning on cable television, every afternoon on the stock market report, every weekend in *Barron's*, every week in dozens of market newsletters, and whenever businesspeople get together, there is rampant conjecture on where the market is heading. Many speculators attempt to predict the market direction by using technical analysis— past stock price fluctuations—as a guide. Technical analysis is based on the presumption that past share price meanderings, rather than underlying business value, hold the key to future stock prices. In reality, no one knows what the market will do; trying to predict it is a waste of time, and investing based upon that prediction is a speculative undertaking.

Market participants do not wear badges that identify them as investors or speculators. It is sometimes difficult to tell the two apart without studying their behavior at length. Examining what they own is not a giveaway, for any security can be owned by investors, speculators, or both. Indeed, many "investment professionals" actually perform as speculators much of the time because of the way they define their mission, pursuing short-term trading profits from predictions of market fluctuations rather than long-term investment profits based on business fundamentals. As we shall see, investors have a reasonable chance of achieving long-term investment success; speculators, by contrast, are likely to lose money over time.

Trading Sardines and Eating Sardines: The Essence of Speculation

> There is the old story about the market craze in sardine trading when the sardines disappeared from their traditional waters in Monterey, California. The commodity traders bid them up and the price of a can of sardines soared. One day a buyer decided to treat himself to an expensive meal and actually opened a can and started eating. He immediately became ill and told the seller the sardines were no good. The seller said, "You don't understand. These are not eating sardines, they are trading sardines."[1]

Like sardine traders, many financial-market participants are attracted to speculation, never bothering to taste the sardines they are trading. Speculation offers the prospect of instant gratification; why get rich slowly if you can get rich quickly? Moreover, speculation involves going along with the crowd, not against it. There is comfort in consensus; those in the majority gain confidence from their very number.

Today many financial-market participants, knowingly or unknowingly, have become speculators. They may not even realize that they are playing a "greater-fool game," buying overvalued securities and expecting—hoping—to find someone, a greater fool, to buy from them at a still higher price.

There is great allure to treating stocks as pieces of paper that you trade. Viewing stocks this way requires neither rigorous analysis nor knowledge of the underlying businesses. Moreover, trading in and of itself can be exciting and, as long as the market is rising, lucrative. But essentially it is speculating, not investing. You may find a buyer at a higher price—a greater fool—or you may not, in which case you yourself are the greater fool.

Value investors pay attention to financial reality in making their investment decisions. Speculators have no such tether. Since many of today's market participants are speculators and not investors, business fundamentals are not necessarily a limiting factor in securities pricing. The resulting propensity of the stock market to periodically become and remain overvalued is all the more reason for fundamental investors to be careful, avoiding any overpriced investments that will require selling to another, even greater fool.

Speculative activity can erupt on Wall Street at any time and is not usually recognized as such until considerable time has passed and much money has been lost. In the middle of 1983, to cite one example, the capital markets assigned a combined market value of over $5 billion to twelve publicly traded, venture-capital-backed Winchester disk-drive manufacturers. Between 1977 and 1984 forty-three different manufacturers of Winchester disk drives received venture-capital financing. A Harvard Business School study entitled "Capital Market Myopia"[2] calculated that industry fundamentals (as of mid-1983) could not then nor in the foreseeable future have justified the total market capitalization of these companies. The study determined that a few firms might ultimately succeed and dominate the industry, while many of the others would struggle or fail. The high potential returns from the winners, if any emerged, would not offset the losses from the others. While investors at the time may not have realized it, the shares of these disk-drive companies were essentially "trading sardines." This speculative bubble burst soon thereafter, with the total market capitalization of these companies declining from $5.4 billion in mid-1983 to $1.5 billion at year-end 1984. Another example of such speculative activity took place in September 1989. The shares of the Spain Fund, Inc., a closed-end mutual fund investing in publicly traded Spanish securities, were bid up in price from approximately net asset value (NAV)—the combined market value of the underlying investments divided by the number of shares outstanding—to more than twice that level. Much of the buying emanated from Japan, where underlying value was evidently less important to investors than other considerations. Although an identical portfolio to that owned by the Spain Fund could have been freely purchased on the Spanish stock market for half the price of Spain Fund shares, these Japanese speculators were not deterred. The Spain Fund priced at twice net asset value was another example of trading sardines; the only possible reason for buying the Spain Fund rather than the underlying securities was the belief that its shares would appreciate to an even more overpriced level. Within months of the speculative advance the share price plunged back to prerally levels, once again approximating the NAV, which itself had never significantly fluctuated.

For still another example of speculation on Wall Street, consider the U.S. government bond market in which traders buy and sell billions of dollars' worth of thirty-year U.S. Treasury bonds every day. Even long-term investors seldom hold thirty-year government bonds to maturity. According to Albert Wojnilower, the average holding period of U.S. Treasury bonds with maturities of ten years or more is only twenty days.[3] Professional traders and so-called investors alike prize thirty-year Treasury bonds for their liquidity and use them to speculate on short-term interest rate movements, while never contemplating the prospect of actually holding them to maturity. Yet someone who buys long-term securities intending to quickly resell rather than hold is a speculator, and thirty-year Treasury bonds have also effectively become trading sardines. We can all wonder what would happen if the thirty-year Treasury bond fell from favor as a speculative vehicle, causing these short-term holders to rush to sell at once and turning thirty-year Treasury bonds back into eating sardines.

Investments and Speculations

Just as financial-market participants can be divided into two groups, investors and speculators, assets and securities can often be characterized as either investments or speculations. The distinction is not clear to most people. Both investments and speculations can be bought and sold. Both typically fluctuate in price and can thus appear to generate investment returns. But there is one critical difference: investments throw off cash flow for the benefit of the owners; speculations do not.[4] The return to the owners of speculations depends exclusively on the vagaries of the resale market.

The greedy tendency to want to own anything that has recently been rising in price lures many people into purchasing speculations. Stocks and bonds go up and down in price, as do Monets and Mickey Mantle rookie cards, but there should be no confusion as to which are the true investments. Collectibles, such as art, antiques, rare coins, and baseball cards, are not investments, but rank speculations. This may not be of consequence to the Chase Manhattan Bank, which in the late 1980s formed a fund for its clients to invest in art, or to David L. Paul, former chairman of the now insolvent CenTrust Savings and Loan Association, who spent $13 million of the thrift's money to purchase just one painting. Even Wall Street, which knows better, chooses at times to blur the distinction. Salomon Brothers, for example, now publishes the rate of return on various asset classes, including in the same list U.S. Treasury bills, stocks, impressionist and old master paintings, and Chinese ceramics. In Salomon's June 1989 rankings the latter categories were ranked at the top of the list, far outdistancing the returns from true investments.

Investments, even very long-term investments like newly planted timber properties, will eventually throw off cash flow. A machine makes widgets that are marketed, a building is occupied by tenants who pay rent, and trees on a timber property are eventually harvested and sold. By contrast, collectibles throw off no cash flow; the only cash they can generate is from their eventual sale. The future buyer is likewise dependent on his or her own prospects for resale.

The value of collectibles, therefore, fluctuates solely with supply and demand. Collectibles have not historically been recognized as stores of value, thus their prices depend on the vagaries of taste, which are certainly subject to change. The apparent value of collectibles is based on circular reasoning: people buy because others have recently bought. This has the effect of bidding up prices, which attracts publicity and creates the illusion of attractive returns. Such logic can fail at any time.

Investment success requires an appropriate mind-set. Investing is serious business, not entertainment. If you participate in the financial markets at all, it is crucial to do so as an investor, not as a speculator, and to be certain that you understand the difference. Needless to say, investors are able to distinguish Pepsico from Picasso and understand the difference between an investment and a collectible. When your hard-earned savings and future financial security are at stake, the cost of not distinguishing is unacceptably high.

The Differences between Successful and Unsuccessful Investors

Successful investors tend to be unemotional, allowing the greed and fear of others to play into their hands. By having confidence in their own analysis and judgment, they respond to market forces not with blind emotion but with calculated reason. Successful investors, for example, demonstrate caution in frothy markets and steadfast conviction in panicky ones. Indeed, the very way an investor views the market and its price fluctuations is a key factor in his or her ultimate investment success or failure.

Taking Advantage of Mr. Market

I wrote earlier that financial-market participants must choose between investment and speculation. Those who (wisely) choose investment are faced with another choice, this time between two opposing views of the financial markets. One view, widely held among academics and increasingly among institutional investors, is that the financial markets are efficient and that trying to outperform the averages is futile. Matching the market return is the best you can hope for. Those who attempt to outperform the market will incur high transaction costs and taxes, causing them to underperform instead.

The other view is that some securities are inefficiently priced, creating opportunities for investors to profit with low risk. This view was perhaps best expressed by Benjamin Graham, who posited the existence of a Mr. Market.[5] An ever helpful fellow, Mr. Market stands ready every business day to buy or sell a vast array of securities in virtually limitless quantities at prices that he sets. He provides this valuable service free of charge. Sometimes Mr. Market sets prices at levels where you would neither want to buy nor sell. Frequently, however, he becomes irrational. Sometimes he is optimistic and will pay far more than securities are worth. Other times he is pessimistic, offering to sell securities for considerably less than underlying value. Value investors—who buy at a discount from underlying value—are in a position to take advantage of Mr. Market's irrationality.

Some investors—really speculators—mistakenly look to Mr. Market for investment guidance. They observe him setting a lower price for a security and, unmindful of his irrationality, rush to sell their holdings, ignoring their own assessment of underlying value. Other times they see him raising prices and, trusting his lead, buy in at the higher figure *as if he knew more than they.* The reality is that Mr. Market knows nothing, being the product of the collective action of thousands of buyers and sellers who themselves are not always motivated by investment fundamentals. Emotional investors and speculators inevitably lose money; investors who take advantage of Mr. Market's periodic irrationality, by contrast, have a good chance of enjoying long-term success.

Mr. Market's daily fluctuations may seem to provide feedback for investors' recent decisions. For a recent purchase decision rising prices provide positive reinforcement; falling prices, negative reinforcement. If you buy a stock that subsequently rises in price, it is easy to allow the positive feedback provided by Mr. Market to influence your judgment. You may start to believe that the security is worth more than you previously thought and refrain from selling, effectively placing the judgment of Mr. Market above your own. You may even decide to buy more shares of this stock, anticipating Mr. Market's future movements. As long as the price appears to be rising, you may choose to hold, perhaps even ignoring deteriorating business fundamentals or a diminution in underlying value.

Similarly, when the price of a stock declines after its initial purchase, most investors, somewhat naturally, become concerned. They start to worry that Mr. Market may know more than they do or that their original assessment was in error. It is easy to panic and sell at just the wrong time. Yet if the security were truly a bargain when it was purchased, the rational course of action would be to take advantage of this even better bargain and buy more.

Louis Lowenstein has warned us not to confuse the real success of an investment with its mirror of success in the stock market.[6] The fact that a stock price rises does not ensure that the underlying business is doing well or that the price increase is justified by a corresponding increase in underlying value. Likewise, a price fall in and of itself does not necessarily reflect adverse business developments or value deterioration.

It is vitally important for investors to distinguish stock price fluctuations from underlying business reality. If the general tendency is for buying to beget more buying and selling to precipitate more selling, investors must fight the tendency to capitulate to market forces. You cannot ignore the market—ignoring a source of investment opportunities would obviously be a mistake—but you must think for yourself and not allow the market to direct you. Value in relation to price, not price alone, must determine your investment decisions. If you look to Mr. Market as a creator of investment opportunities (where price departs from underlying value), you have the makings of a value investor. If you insist on looking to Mr. Market for investment guidance, however, you are probably best advised to hire someone else to manage your money.

Security prices move up and down for two basic reasons: to

reflect business reality (or investor perceptions of that reality) or to reflect short-term variations in supply and demand. Reality can change in a number of ways, some company-specific, others macroeconomic in nature. If Coca-Cola's business expands or prospects improve and the stock price increases proportionally, the rise may simply reflect an increase in business value. If Aetna's share price plunges when a hurricane causes billions of dollars in catastrophic losses, a decline in total market value approximately equal to the estimated losses may be appropriate. When the shares of Fund American Companies, Inc., surge as a result of the unexpected announcement of the sale of its major subsidiary, Fireman's Fund Insurance Company, at a very high price, the price increase reflects the sudden and nearly complete realization of underlying value. On a macroeconomic level a broad-based decline in interest rates, a drop in corporate tax rates, or a rise in the expected rate of economic growth could each precipitate a general increase in security prices.

Security prices sometimes fluctuate, not based on any apparent changes in reality, but on changes in investor perception. The shares of many biotechnology companies doubled and tripled in the first months of 1991, for example despite a lack of change in company or industry fundamentals that could possibly have explained that magnitude of increase. The only explanation for the price rise was that investors were suddenly willing to pay much more than before to buy the same thing.

In the short run supply and demand alone determine market prices. If there are many large sellers and few buyers, prices fall, sometimes beyond reason. Supply-and-demand imbalances can result from year-end tax selling, an institutional stampede out of a stock that just reported disappointing earnings, or an unpleasant rumor. Most day-to-day market price fluctuations result from supply-and-demand variations rather than from fundamental developments.

Investors will frequently not know why security prices fluctuate. They may change because of, in the absence of, or in complete indifference to changes in underlying value. In the short run investor perception may be as important as reality itself in determining security prices. It is never clear which future events are anticipated by investors and thus already reflected in today's security prices. Because security prices can change for any number of reasons and because it is impossible to know what expectations are reflected in any given price level, investors must look beyond security prices to underlying business value, always comparing the two as part of the investment process.

Unsuccessful Investors and Their Costly Emotions

Unsuccessful investors are dominated by emotion. Rather than responding coolly and rationally to market fluctuations, they respond emotionally with greed and fear. We all know people who act responsibly and deliberately most of the time but go berserk when investing money. It may take them many months, even years, of hard work and disciplined saving to accumulate the money but only a few minutes to invest it. The same people would read several consumer publications and visit numerous stores before purchasing a stereo or camera yet spend little or no time investigating the stock they just heard about from a friend. Rationality that is applied to the purchase of electronic or photographic equipment is absent when it comes to investing.

Many unsuccessful investors regard the stock market as a way to make money without working rather than as a way to invest capital in order to earn a decent return. Anyone would enjoy a quick and easy profit, and the prospect of an effortless gain incites greed in investors. Greed leads many investors to seek shortcuts to investment success. Rather than allowing returns to compound over time, they attempt to turn quick profits by acting on hot tips. They do not stop to consider how the tipster could possibly be in possession of valuable information that is not illegally obtained or why, if it is so valuable, it is being made available to them. Greed also manifests itself as undue optimism or, more subtly, as complacency in the face of bad news. Finally greed can cause investors to shift their focus away from the achievement of long-term investment goals in favor of short-term speculation.

High levels of greed sometimes cause new-era thinking to be introduced by market participants to justify buying or holding overvalued securities. Reasons are given as to why this time is different from anything that came before. As the truth is stretched, investor behavior is carried to an extreme. Conservative assumptions are revisited and revised in order to justify ever higher prices, and a mania can ensue. In the short run resisting the mania is not only psychologically but also financially difficult as the participants make a lot of money, at least on paper. Then, predictably, the mania reaches a peak, is recognized for what it is, reverses course, and turns into a selling panic. Greed gives way to fear, and investor losses can be enormous.

As I discuss later in detail, junk bonds were definitely such a mania. Prior to the 1980s the entire junk-bond market consisted of only a few billion dollars of "fallen angels." Although newly issued junk bonds were a 1980s invention and were thus untested over a full economic cycle, they became widely accepted as a financial innovation of great importance, with total issuance exceeding $200 billion. Buyers greedily departed from historical standards of business valuation and creditworthiness. Even after the bubble burst, many proponents stubbornly clung to the validity of the concept.

Greed and the Yield Pigs of the 1980s

There are countless examples of investor greed in recent financial history. Few, however, were as relentless as the decade-long "reach for yield" of the 1980s. Double-digit interest rates on U.S. government securities early in the decade whetted investors' appetites for high nominal returns. When interest rates declined to single digits, many investors remained infatuated with the attainment of higher yields and sacrificed credit quality to achieve them either in the bond market or in equities. Known

among Wall Streeters as "yield pigs" (or a number of more deri-
sive names), such individual and institutional investors were
susceptible to any investment product that promised a high rate
of return. Wall Street responded with gusto, as Wall Street tends
to do when there are fees to earn, creating a variety of instruments that promised high current yields.

U.S. government securities are generally regarded as "risk-
free" investments, at least insofar as credit quality is concerned.
To achieve current cash yields appreciably above those available from U.S. government securities, investors must either risk
the loss of principal or incur its certain depletion. Low-grade
securities, such as junk bonds, offer higher yields than government bonds but at the risk of principal loss. Junk-bond mutual
funds were marketed to investors in the 1980s primarily
through the promise of high current yield. As with a magician
performing sleight of hand, investors' eyes were focused almost
exclusively on the attractive current yield, while the high principal risk from defaults was hidden from view.

Junk bonds were not the only slop served up to the yield pigs
of the 1980s. Wall Street found many ways to offer investors an
enhanced current yield by incorporating a return of the
investors' principal into the reported yield. "Ginnie Maes,"
which are, in fact, high-grade securities, are one such example.
These are pools of mortgages insured by the Government
National Mortgage Association (GNMA, whence Ginnie Mae), a
U.S. government agency. GNMA pools collect mortgage interest
and principal payments from homeowners and distribute them
to bondholders. Every month owners of GNMAs receive distributions that include both interest income and small principal
repayments. The principal portion includes contractual payments as well as voluntary prepayments. Many holders tend to
think of the yield on GNMAs in terms of the total monthly distribution received. The true economic yield is, in fact, only the
interest payments received divided by the outstanding principal
balance. The principal component of the monthly distributions is
not a yield *on* capital, but a return *of* capital. Thus investors who
spend the entire cash flow are eating into their seed corn.

The same principle is operative in option-income mutual

funds, which typically acquire a portfolio of U.S. government securities and then write (sell) call options against them. (A call option is the right to buy a security at a specified price during a stated period of time.) The cash distributions paid by these funds to shareholders are comprised of both interest income earned on the bond portfolio and premiums generated from the sale of options. This total cash distribution is touted as the current yield to investors. When covered call options written against the portfolio are exercised, however, the writer forgoes appreciation on the securities that are called away. The upside potential on the underlying investments is truncated by the sale of the call options, while the downside risk remains intact. This strategy places investors in the position of uninsured homeowners, who benefit currently from the small premium not paid to the insurance company while remaining exposed to large future losses. As long as security prices continue to fluctuate both up and down, writers of covered calls are certain to experience capital losses over time, with no possible offsetting capital gains. In effect, these funds are eating into principal while misleadingly reporting the principal erosion as yield.

Some investors, fixated on current return, reach for yield not with a new Wall Street product, but a very old one: common stocks. Finding bond yields unacceptably low, they pour money into stocks at the worst imaginable times. These investors fail to consider that bond market yields are public information, well known to stock investors who incorporate the current level of interest rates into share prices. When bond yields are low, share prices are likely to be high. Yield-seeking investors who rush into stocks when yields are low not only fail to achieve a free lunch, they also tend to buy in at or near a market top.

The Search for an Investment Formula

Many investors greedily persist in the investment world's version of a search for the holy grail: the attempt to find a successful investment formula. It is human nature to seek simple solutions to problems, however complex. Given the complexities of the investment process, it is perhaps natural for people to feel that only a formula could lead to investment success.

Just as many generals persist in fighting the last war, most investment formulas project the recent past into the future. Some investment formulas involve technical analysis, in which past stock-price movements are considered predictive of future prices. Other formulas incorporate investment fundamentals such as price-to-earnings (P/E) ratios, price-to-book-value ratios, sales or profits growth rates, dividend yields, and the prevailing level of interest rates. Despite the enormous effort that has been put into devising such formulas, none has been proven to work.

One simplistic, backward-looking formula employed by some investors is to buy stocks with low P/E ratios. The idea is that by paying a low multiple of earnings, an investor is buying an out-of-favor bargain. In reality investors who follow such a formula are essentially driving by looking only in the rear-view mirror. Stocks with a low P/E ratio are often depressed because the market price has already discounted the prospect of a sharp fall in earnings. Investors who buy such stocks may soon find that the P/E ratio has risen because earnings have declined.

Another type of formula used by many investors involves projecting their most recent personal experiences into the future. As a result, many investors have entered the 1990s having "learned" a number of wrong and potentially dangerous lessons from the ebullient 1980s market performance; some have come to regard the 1987 stock market crash as nothing more than an aberration and nothing less than a great buying opportunity. The quick recovery after the October 1989 stock market shakeout and 1990 junk-bond market collapse provide reinforcement of this shortsighted lesson. Many investors, like Pavlov's dog, will foolishly look to the next market selloff, regardless of its proximate cause, as another buying "opportunity."

The financial markets are far too complex to be incorporated into a formula. Moreover, if any successful investment formula could be devised, it would be exploited by those who possessed it until competition eliminated the excess profits. The quest for a formula that worked would then begin anew. Investors would be much better off to redirect the time and effort committed to devising formulas into fundamental analysis of specific investment opportunities.

Conclusion

The financial markets offer many temptations to vulnerable investors. It is easy to do the wrong thing, to speculate rather than invest. Emotion lies dangerously close to the surface for most investors and can be particularly intense when market prices move dramatically in either direction. It is crucial that investors understand the difference between speculating and investing and learn to take advantage of the opportunities presented by Mr. Market.

Notes

1. Sequoia Fund, Inc., annual report for 1986.
2. William A. Sahlman and Howard H. Stevenson (Harvard Graduate School of Business Administration Case Study), "Capital Market Myopia" (Cambridge: Harvard Business School, 1985).
3. Albert Wojnilower, quoted in Louis Lowenstein, *What's Wrong with Wall Street* (Reading, Mass.: Addison-Wesley, 1988), p. 75.
4. The only *possible* exceptions to this cash flow test are precious metals, such as gold, which is a widely recognized store of value; throughout history, for instance, the value of an ounce of gold has been roughly equivalent to the cost of a fine men's suit. Other precious metals and gems have a less-established value than gold but might be considered by some to be a similar type of holding.
5. Benjamin Graham, *The Intelligent Investor*, 4th ed. (New York: Harper & Row, 1973), p. 108.
6. Lowenstein, *What's Wrong with Wall Street*, p. 37.

2

The Nature of Wall Street
Works Against Investors

Investors in marketable securities have little choice but to deal with Wall Street. The sad truth is, however, that many investors are not well served in their dealings with Wall Street; they would benefit from developing a greater understanding of the way Wall Street works. The problem is that what is good for Wall Street is not necessarily good for investors, and vice versa.

Wall Street has three principal activities: trading, investment banking, and merchant banking. As traders Wall Street firms act as agents, earning a commission (or trading spread) for bringing buyers and sellers together. As investment bankers they arrange for the purchase and sale of entire companies by others, underwrite new securities, provide financial advice, and opine on the fairness of specific transactions. As merchant bankers they commit their own capital while acting as principal in investment banking transactions. Merchant banking activity became increasingly important to Wall Street in the late 1980s but almost completely ceased in 1990 and early 1991.

Wall Street firms perform important functions for our economy: they raise capital for expanding businesses and (sometimes) provide liquidity to markets. As Wall Street pursues its various activities, however, it frequently is plagued by conflicts of interest and a short-term orientation. Investors need not condemn Wall Street for this as long as they remain aware of it and act with cautious skepticism in any interactions they may have.

Up-Front Fees and Commissions: Wall Street's Primary Conflict of Interest

Wall Streeters get paid primarily for what they do, not how effectively they do it. Wall Street's traditional compensation is in the form of up-front fees and commissions. Brokerage commissions are collected on each trade, regardless of the outcome for the investor. Investment banking and underwriting fees are also collected up front, long before the ultimate success or failure of the transaction is known.

All investors are aware of the conflict of interest facing stockbrokers. While their customers might be best off owning (minimal commission) U.S. Treasury bills or (commission-free) no-load mutual funds, brokers are financially motivated to sell high-commission securities. Brokers also have an incentive to do excessive short-term trading (known as churning) on behalf of discretionary customer accounts (in which the broker has discretion to transact) and to encourage such activity in nondiscretionary accounts. Many investors are also accustomed to conflicts of interest in Wall Street's trading activities, where the firm and customer are on opposite sides of what is often a zero-sum game.

A significant conflict of interest also arises in securities underwriting. This function involves raising money for corporate clients by selling newly issued securities to customers. Needless to say, large fees may motivate a firm to underwrite either overpriced or highly risky securities and to favor the limited number of underwriting clients over the many small buyers of those securities.

In merchant banking the conflict is more blatant still. Wall

Street firms have become direct competitors of both their underwriting and brokerage clients, buying and selling entire companies or large corporate subsidiaries for their own accounts. Instead of acting as middlemen between issuers and buyers of securities, firms have become issuers and investors themselves. Nowadays when the phone rings and your broker is on the line, you don't even know in what capacity or on whose behalf he or she is acting.

Obviously there is nothing wrong with providing a service and collecting a fee. Doctors, lawyers, accountants, and other professionals are paid this way; their compensation does not depend on the ultimate outcome of their services. The point I am making is that investors should be aware of the motivations of the people they transact business with; up-front fees clearly create a bias toward frequent, and not necessarily profitable, transactions.

Wall Street Favors Underwritings over Secondary-Market Transactions

By acting as investment bankers as well as brokers, most Wall Street firms create their own products to sell. A stock or bond underwriting generates high fees for an investment bank. These are shared with stockbrokers who sell the underwritten securities to clients. The total Wall Street take from a stock underwriting, for example, ranges from 2 to 8 percent of the proceeds raised; the brokers themselves typically receive fifteen to thirty cents of gross commission on a $10 stock.

By contrast, the commissions earned by brokers on secondary-market transactions, which involve the resale of securities from one investor to another, are much smaller. Large institutions generally pay as little as five cents per share and sometimes as low as two cents. Small individual investors are typically charged considerably more. Even so, brokers earn on average several times more money from selling shares in a new underwriting than they can earn from a secondary-market transaction of similar size. The higher commission on new underwritings provides a strong incentive to stockbrokers to sell them to clients.

The strong financial incentive of brokers touting new security underwritings is not the only cause for investor concern. The motivation of the issuer of securities is also suspect and must be thoroughly investigated by the buyer. Gone are the days (if they ever existed) when a new issue was a collaborative effort in which a business that was long on prospects but short on capital could meet investors with capital in hand but with few good outlets for it. Today the initial public offering market is where hopes and dreams are capitalized at high multiples. Indeed, the underwriting of a new security may well be an overpriced or ill-conceived transaction, frequently involving the shuffling of assets through "financial engineering" rather than the raising of capital to finance a business's internal growth.

Investors even remotely tempted to buy new issues must ask themselves how they could possibly fare well when a savvy issuer and greedy underwriter are on the opposite side of every underwriting. Indeed, how attractive could any security underwriting ever be when the issuer and underwriter have superior information as well as control over the timing, pricing, and stock or bond allocation? The deck is almost always stacked against the buyers.

Sometimes the lust for underwriting fees drives Wall Street to actually create underwriting clients for the sole purpose of having securities to sell. Most closed-end mutual funds, for example, are formed almost exclusively to generate commissions for stockbrokers and fees for investment managers. There was a story a few years ago that an announcement to the sales force of a prestigious Wall Street underwriting firm regarding the formation of a closed-end bond fund was met with a standing ovation. The clients could have purchased the same securities much less expensively on a direct basis, but in the form of a closed-end fund the brokers stood to make many times more in commissions.

Closed-end mutual funds are typically offered initially to investors at $10 per share; an 8 percent commission is paid to the underwriter, leaving $9.20 to invest. Within months of issuance, closed-end funds typically decline in price below the initial per share net asset value (the market value of the underlying holdings) of $9.20. This means that purchasers of closed-end funds on the initial public offering frequently incur a quick loss of 10 to 15 percent of their investment. From the initial purchasers' perspective the same purpose could be achieved less expensively through existing no-load open-end mutual funds. These funds are able to make the same investments as closed-end funds but no underwriting fee or sales charge is paid; unlike closed-end funds, they can always be bought and sold at net asset value (NAV).[1]

The 1989–90 boom in the creation of new closed-end country funds exemplifies the tension between Wall Street and its customers. As noted in chapter 1, speculative interest in closed-end country funds resulted in the shares of many funds being bid far above underlying NAVs. Buying into new offerings appeared to be a quick, easy, and almost certain way to make money. In June 1989, for example, the Spain Fund, Inc., sold at 92 percent of NAV, an 8 percent discount. Only three months later the shares traded at more than 260 percent of NAV and remained at more than twice NAV until February 1990. By late summer of that year the share price once again approximated NAV, which was somewhat lower than it had been a year earlier. This price trend is not unique; the share prices of several other country funds underwent similar gyrations.

Investor enthusiasm for country funds was bolstered by the sudden collapse of communism and the democratization of Eastern Europe; peace appeared to be "breaking out" around the world. Funds were formed to invest in such exotic locales as Austria, Brazil, Ireland, Thailand, and Turkey. Ironically, only months after the boom in issuance of closed-end country funds peaked, Iraq invaded Kuwait. The price of oil rose sharply, recession fears mounted, and stock markets worldwide plunged. The prospect of finding new buyers who would pay even greater premiums to NAV suddenly dimmed. As a result, newly bearish investors dumped the shares of country funds, which had recently traded at large premiums to NAV, until virtually all of them declined to levels appreciably below NAV.

The periodic boom in closed-end mutual-fund issuance is a useful barometer of market sentiment; new issues abound when investors are optimistic and markets are rising. Wall Street firms after all do not force investors to buy these funds. They simply stand ready to issue a virtually limitless supply since the only real constraint is the gullibility of the buyers. The boom is followed by a bust, during which those funds that fall to a sufficiently large discount to NAV are targeted by investor groups and either liquidated or forced to become open-ended, thereby permitting the shares to be redeemable at NAV, completing the life cycles of these entities. The underwriters and sometimes the bargain hunters profit; the greater fools who buy on the initial public offerings or later at large premiums to NAV inevitably lose money.

Wall Street's Short-Term Focus

Wall Street's up-front-fee orientation makes for a short-term focus as well. Brokers, traders, and investment bankers all find it hard to look beyond the next transaction when the current one is so lucrative regardless of merit. This was even more applicable than usual in the late 1980s and early 1990s, a time when fees were enormous and when most Wall Streeters felt less than secure about the permanence of their jobs, and even their careers, in the securities industry. The utter hypocrisy of Wall Street is exemplified by the "equitization" wave of early 1991, whereby overleveraged companies issued equity and used the proceeds to repay debt. Wall Street collected investment banking and underwriting fees when those companies were acquired in highly leveraged junk-bond-financed takeovers and collected large fees again when the debt was replaced with newly underwritten equity.

Some people work on Wall Street solely to earn high incomes, expecting to depart after a few years. Others, doubting their own ultimate success, perhaps justifiably, are unwilling to forego short-term compensation for long-term income that may never arrive. The compensation figures are so large that even a few good years on Wall Street can ensure a person's financial security for life.

Notwithstanding, a minority of people on Wall Street have maintained a long-term perspective. A few Wall Street partnerships have done a particularly good job of motivating their employees to think past the current transaction. However, a great many of those who work on Wall Street view the goodwill or financial success of clients as a secondary consideration; short-term maximization of their own income is the primary goal.

Many Wall Streeters, especially stockbrokers, have come to believe that their clients will normally leave them after a couple of years, in effect rationalizing their own short-term orientations by blaming their clients. There are no sure things on Wall Street, and even the best-intentioned and most insightful advice may not work out. It is true that clients who incur losses may switch brokers. This does not excuse those who assume that client turnover is the norm and thus seek to maximize commissions and fees over the short term, making client turnover a self-fulfilling prophecy.

Wall Street's Bullish Bias

Investors must never forget that Wall Street has a strong bullish bias, which coincides with its self-interest. Wall Street firms can complete more security underwritings in good markets than in bad. Brokers, likewise, do more business and have happier customers in a rising market. Even securities held in inventory to facilitate trading tend to increase in price during bull markets. When a Wall Street analyst or broker expresses optimism, investors must take it with a grain of salt.

The bullish bias of Wall Street manifests itself in many ways. Wall Street research is strongly oriented toward buy rather than sell recommendations, for example. Perhaps this is the case because anyone with money is a candidate to buy a stock or bond, while only those who own are candidates to sell. In other words, there is more brokerage business to be done by issuing an optimistic research report than by writing a pessimistic one.

In addition, Wall Street analysts are unlikely to issue sell recommendations due to an understandable reluctance to say negative things, however truthful they may be, about the companies they follow. This is especially true when these companies are corporate-finance clients of the firm. In 1990 Marvin Roffman, an analyst at Janney Montgomery Scott, Inc., apparently lost his job for writing a negative research report about the Atlantic City hotel/casinos owned by Donald Trump, a prospective client of Janney.

It is easy for Wall Streeters to be bullish. A few optimistic assumptions will enable a reasonable investment case to be made for practically any stock or bond. The problem is that with so much attention being paid to the upside, it is easy to lose sight of the risk.

Others share Wall Street's bullish bias. Investors naturally prefer rising security prices to falling ones, profits to losses. It is more pleasant to contemplate upside potential than downside risk. Companies too prefer to see their own shares rise in price; an increasing share price is viewed as a vote of confidence in management, as a source of increase in the value of management's personal shares and stock options, and as a source of financial flexibility, facilitating a company's ability to raise additional equity capital.

Even government regulators of the securities markets have a stake in the markets' bullish bias. Rising markets are accompanied by investor confidence, which the regulators desire to maintain. Any downturn, according to the regulatory mentality, should be orderly and free of panic. (Disorderly rising markets are of no evident concern.)

Accordingly, market regulators have devised certain stock market rules that have the effect of exacerbating the upward bias of Wall Streeters. First, many institutions, including all mutual funds, are prohibited from selling stocks or bonds short. (A short sale involves selling borrowed stocks or bonds; it is the opposite of the traditional investment strategy of buying a security, otherwise known as going long.) Second, while there are no restrictions on buying a stock, the short sale of exchange-listed stocks requires physically borrowing the desired number of shares and then executing a sell order on an "uptick" (an upward price fluctuation) from the preceding trade.[2] This can greatly limit investors' ability to execute short-sale transactions. The combination of restrictive short-sale rules and the limited number of investors who are both willing and able to accept the unlimited downside risk of short-selling increases the likelihood that security prices may become overvalued. Short-sellers, who might otherwise step in to correct an overvaluation, are few in number and significantly constrained.[3]

After the October 1987 stock market crash several "circuit breakers" were introduced to limit downward price swings on a given day. These included restrictions on the price movement of stocks and index futures and on program trading.[4] The effect of circuit breakers ranges from a temporary halt in futures trading to a complete market shutdown.

Two New York Stock Exchange circuit breakers apply only to market declines. If the Dow Jones Industrial Average falls 250 points below the previous day's close, trading is stopped for one hour. If stocks fall another 150 points after trading resumes, there will be an additional two-hour halt. It is noteworthy that there is no similar provision regarding upward price movements, regardless of magnitude. This is another example of how the rules favor bulls over bears and militate toward higher stock prices. Although high stock prices cannot be legislated (something that many on Wall Street may secretly wish), regulation can cause overvaluation to persist by making it easier to occur and more difficult to correct. The upward bias of market regulators, illustrated by the uneven application of circuit breakers, may itself encourage investors to purchase and hold overvalued securities.

Many of the same factors that contribute to a bullish bias can cause the financial markets, especially the stock market, to become and remain overvalued. Correcting a market overvaluation is more difficult than remedying an undervalued condition. With an undervalued stock, for example, a value investor can purchase more and more shares until control is achieved or, better still, until the entire company is owned at a bargain price. If the value assessment was accurate, this is an attractive outcome for the investor. By contrast, overvalued markets are not easily corrected; short-selling, as mentioned earlier, is not an effective antidote. In addition, overvaluation is not always apparent to investors, analysts, or managements. Since security prices reflect investors' perception of reality and not necessarily reality itself, overvaluation may persist for a long time.

Financial-Market Innovations Are Good for Wall Street But Bad for Clients

Investment bankers in Wall Street firms are constantly creating new types of securities to offer to customers. Occasionally such offerings both solve the financial problems of issuers and meet the needs of investors. In most cases, however, they address only the needs of Wall Street, that is, the generation of fees and commissions.

Financial intermediaries—Wall Street investment bankers and institutional investors—stand to benefit the most from financial-market innovations. Wall Street earns fees and commissions with no risk; institutional investors may be able to attract more money to manage by creating new vehicles to invest in the innovative securities. If the first investors in a financial-market innovation experience good results, more money will be raised and more securities will be issued, generating additional management fees, underwriting fees, and commissions. The buy side and sell side in effect become co-conspirators, each having a vested interest in the continued success of the innovation. Any long-term benefit to the issuers or actual owners of the new securities is considerably less certain.

In the 1980s the financial markets were flooded with new varieties of debt and derivative securities. Just to name a few, an investor could buy bonds that were fixed or floating rate, Dutch auction, zero-coupon, pay-in-kind or pay-in-stock, convertible into the issuers' stock, into someone else's stock, or into commodities, puttable, callable, resettable, extendible to a longer maturity, exchangeable into another security, or denominated in a foreign currency or market basket of currencies. Some of these securities, such as auction-rate preferred-stock and zero-coupon junk bonds, have been discredited by events. Many others, like exhibits at a science fair, may have achieved their original goals, but almost no one really cared.

Investors must recognize that the early success of an innovation is not a reliable indicator of its ultimate merit. Both buyers and sellers must believe that they will benefit in the short run, or the innovation will not get off the drawing board; the longer-term consequences of such innovations, however, may not have been considered carefully. At the time of issuance a new type of security will appear to add value in the same way that a new consumer product does. There is something—lower risk, higher return, greater liquidity, an imbedded put or call option to the holder or issuer, or some other wrinkle—that makes it appear superior (new and improved, if you will) to anything that came before. Although the benefits are apparent from the start, it takes longer for problems to surface. Neither cash-hungry issuers nor greedy investors necessarily analyze the performance of each financial-market innovation under every conceivable economic scenario. What appears to be new and improved today may prove to be flawed or even fallacious tomorrow.

Wall Street is never satisfied with its success. If one deal is successfully completed, Wall Street sees this as a sure sign that still another deal can be done. In virtually all financial innovations and investment fads, Wall Street creates additional supply until it equals and then exceeds market demand. The profit motivation of Wall Street firms and the intense competition among them render any other outcome unlikely.

The eventual market saturation of Wall Street fads coincides with a cooling of investor enthusiasm. When a particular sector is in vogue, success is a self-fulfilling prophecy. As buyers bid up prices, they help to justify their original enthusiasm. When prices peak and start to decline, however, the downward movement can also become self-fulfilling. Not only do buyers stop buying, they actually become sellers, aggravating the oversupply problem that marks the peak of every fad.

IOs and POs: Innovations in the Mortgage Securities Market

One financial-market innovation of the mid-1980s involved hybrid mortgage securities known as IOs (interest only) and POs (principal only). IOs and POs were created by separating a pool of mortgages into its two cash-flow components: interest payments and principal repayments.

A conventional mortgage-backed security fluctuates in value inversely to interest rates for two reasons. First, the value of a mortgage declines as interest rates rise because, as with any interest-bearing security, it is worth less when its periodic cash flows are discounted at the new, higher rate. Second, the expected life of a mortgage lengthens with higher interest rates as optional prepayments lessen, so that the relatively less attractive interest payments last for a longer time.

The responses of separate IOs and POs to interest rate changes are very different from those of an intact mortgage-backed security. IOs, interest payments stripped from a pool of mortgages, fluctuate in value for a given change in interest rates in the opposite direction from conventional mortgages. The reason is, if interest rates rise, interest payments on an IO will be received for a longer period. Experience shows that the present value of a larger number of payments is more than that of a smaller number of payments, even at a somewhat higher discount rate. Because of this counterfluctuation, such mortgage investors as thrifts and insurance companies are attracted to IOs as a potential hedge against changes in interest rates. The price of POs, conversely, moves in the same direction as conventional mortgages in response to interest rate changes but with greater volatility. Thus they are potentially useful instruments for anyone wishing to speculate on interest rates.

Wall Street was able to earn substantial fees and trading profits by creating these hybrid securities. The question, as with any financial-market innovation, is whether anyone else was better off, especially after allowing for the commissions, fees, and dealer markups. The buyers, frequently thrifts and insurance companies, were betting on their own ability to understand a brand new security. They needed to understand it better than other market participants, and at least as well as Wall Street, to avoid being exploited. They depended on the emergence of a sustained, liquid market for the securities they bought. And they were implicitly assuming that the two parts were worth at least as much as, and perhaps more than, the whole—clearly an optimistic assumption.

What if IOs or POs failed to trade in a liquid and orderly market with narrow bid/asked spreads? What if accurate and timely information on these securities ceased to be available on a continuing basis? What if interest rate fluctuations rendered each of these securities more volatile than expected? Then holders were in trouble, for it is far easier to separate a mortgage into two parts than it is to glue it back together again. There was no assurance, or even reason to think it likely, that the holder of one piece would be interested in any proposition made by the holder of the other piece to recombine. It was, in other words, possible that the value of the two parts would be less than the value of the whole; at least one and perhaps both pieces could trade at a discount from theoretical underlying value.

Investment Fads

When a particular security catches Wall Street's fancy, billions of dollars' worth may be issued. Securities are not the only things that can come into favor on Wall Street, however; entire industries do as well. During the 1980s such diverse industries as energy, technology, biotechnology, gambling, warehouse shopping, and even defense basked in the limelight for a time. A boom in the issuance of securities for a particular industry can be lucrative for Wall Street since early success in each area attracts throngs of investors. Initial public offerings ensue, and closed-end mutual funds are often formed; investors' assets are shifted into the newly popular area, generating profits for Wall Street that remain long after investor enthusiasm wanes.

Companies that were viewed as having "business franchises" are one such example of a passing fashion of the late 1980s. A "nifty fifty" quickly emerged, several dozen institutional favorites that traded at considerably higher multiples than the rest of the stock market. Investors soon found excuses to characterize almost anything as a franchise. Businesses that barely existed in the early 1980s, such as Silk Greenhouse, Inc. (fake-flower stores) and TCBY (This Country's Best Yogurt) Enterprises, Inc., were claimed by investors in the late 1980s to have considerable franchise value. Each has since fallen from investor favor, and franchise value is no longer mentioned, except disparagingly, when these firms are discussed.

Ironically, many businesses that formerly had real consumer franchises lost them in the 1980s. The skies were not very friendly to Eastern, Pan Am, Continental, or TWA. Crazy Eddie went bankrupt. E. F. Hutton was no longer talking; its customers, no longer listening. B. Altman went out of business, and the Bank of New England was taken over by regulators. Of course, some companies do have valuable business franchises, but these are neither so permanent nor so resilient as many investors believe. Even reasonably healthy companies like Eastman Kodak and American Express, for example, have seen competitors make significant inroads into their franchises in recent years.

Home shopping on television became an instant investment fad in 1986 with the initial public offering of Home Shopping Network, Inc., a company thought by investors to have tremendous growth potential. By early 1987, despite large operating losses, its total stock market capitalization reached $4.2 billion, a level considerably above that of most well-established department store chains operating hundreds of stores. This level of valuation could be justified only under the most optimistic assumptions of revenue growth, profitability, and future business value. Such optimism was not warranted, given the brief operating history and still-to-be-proven profitability of the home shopping industry. The initial enthusiasm turned out to be significantly overblown. Although the company survived, only a year later the stock had dropped more than 90 percent from its all-time high.

The value of a company selling a trendy product, such as television shopping, depends on the profitability of the product, the product life cycle, competitive barriers, and the ability of the company to replicate its current success. Investors are often overly optimistic about the sustainability of a trend, the ultimate degree of market penetration, and the size of profit margins. As a result, the stock market frequently attributes a Coca-Cola multiple to a Cabbage Patch concept.

All market fads come to an end. Security prices eventually become too high, supply catches up with and then exceeds demand, the top is reached, and the downward slide ensues. There will always be cycles of investment fashion and just as surely investors who are susceptible to them.

It is only fair to note that it is not easy to distinguish an investment fad from a real business trend. Indeed, many investment fads originate in real business trends, which deserve to be reflected in stock prices. The fad becomes dangerous, however, when share prices reach levels that are not supported by the conservatively appraised values of the underlying businesses.

Conclusion

Wall Street can be a dangerous place for investors. You have no choice but to do business there, but you must always be on your guard. The standard behavior of Wall Streeters is to pursue maximization of self-interest; the orientation is usually short term. This must be acknowledged, accepted, and dealt with. If you transact business with Wall Street with these caveats in mind, you can prosper. If you depend on Wall Street to help you, investment success may remain elusive.

Notes

1. The only advantage of closed-end over open-end mutual funds is that closed-end funds can be managed without consideration of liquidity needs since they are not subject to shareholder redemptions. This minor advantage does not offset the high up-front commissions charged to initial purchasers of closed-end fund shares.
2. If the last price fluctuation was upward, the next trade at the same price is called a zero-plus tick; short-selling may take place on a zero-plus tick.
3. Many Wall Streeters have a different view of short-selling. They believe that short-sellers are dangerous manipulators of securities prices, driving prices down for their personal financial gain. This prejudice against short-sellers is consistent with Wall Street's interest in maintaining high stock prices.
4. Program trading is an arbitrage activity in which the stocks in an index are purchased and futures contracts on that index are sold, or vice versa, in either event locking in a riskless profit.

3

The Institutional
Performance Derby: The
Client Is the Loser

Growing pools of retirement and endowment funds seeking sound investment outlets led to the most important development in the investment world over the last three decades: the ascendancy of the institutional investor. Unfortunately institutional investing has developed in ways that are detrimental to the returns generated on the money under management. The great majority of institutional investors are plagued with a short-term, relative-performance orientation and lack the long-term perspective that retirement and endowment funds deserve. Myriad rules and restrictions, often self-imposed, also impair the ability of institutional investors to achieve good investment results.

Several decades ago the financial markets were dominated by individual investors who made their own investment decisions. The investment world was then a simpler place; stocks, government bonds, and high-grade corporate bonds comprised virtually the entire investment menu. That world was a cautious one, as memories of the 1929 stock market crash and the Great Depression that followed were slow to fade.

In the years after World War II, however, increasing pools of retirement savings in corporate pension funds created an opportunity for professional money managers to go into business. Total funds under management rose from $107 billion in 1950 to more than $500 billion in 1968, to approximately $2 trillion in 1980, and $6 trillion in 1990. Over the same forty years, the share of institutional ownership in all publicly traded U.S. equity securities increased from 8 to 45 percent.[1]

Under the Employee Retirement Income Security Act of 1974 (ERISA) institutional investors were required to act as fiduciaries for future retirees by achieving acceptable investment returns with limited risk. Adoption of the prudent-man standard, under which pension funds would only make investments that a "prudent man" would make, was intended to ensure conservative management. Over time, however, the *modus operandi* of institutional investors began to diverge from what the statute intended. A 1979 U.S. Department of Labor ruling that the prudent-man standard applied to an entire portfolio rather than to the individual securities within it opened the door to portfolio-oriented investment strategies that ignore risk on an investment-by-investment basis. In addition, a great many institutional investors have been swept into the short-term relative-performance derby, an orientation inconsistent with the prudent-man test.

Today institutional investors dominate the financial markets, accounting for roughly three-fourths of stock exchange trading volume.[2] All investors are affected by what the institutions do, owing to the impact of their enormous financial clout on security prices. Understanding their behavior is helpful in understanding why certain securities are overvalued while others are bargain priced and may enable investors to identify areas of potential opportunity.

The Money Management Business

If the behavior of institutional investors weren't so horrifying, it might actually be humorous. Hundreds of billions of other people's hard-earned dollars are routinely whipped from investment to investment based on little or no in-depth research or analysis. The prevalent mentality is consensus, groupthink. Acting with the crowd ensures an acceptable mediocrity; acting independently runs the risk of unacceptable underperformance. Indeed, the short-term, relative-performance orientation of many money managers has made "institutional investor" a contradiction in terms.

Institutional investors are presumably motivated both by the ongoing challenge of achieving good investment results and by the personal financial success that accrues to participants in a profitable money management business. Unfortunately for investment clients these objectives frequently are at odds. Most money managers are compensated, not according to the results they achieve, but as a percentage of the total assets under management. The incentive is to expand managed assets in order to generate more fees. Yet while a money management business typically becomes more profitable as assets under management increase, good investment performance becomes increasingly difficult. This conflict between the best interests of the money manager and that of the clients is typically resolved in the manager's favor.

The business of money management can be highly lucrative. It requires very little capital investment, while offering high compensation and the rapid development of what is effectively an annuity. Once an investment management business becomes highly profitable, it is likely to remain that way so long as clients do not depart in large numbers. In the money management business management fees paid by new clients constitute almost pure profit. Similarly, lost fees resulting from client departures affect profitability nearly dollar for dollar, since there are few variable costs to be cut in order to offset lost revenues.

The pressure to retain clients exerts a stifling influence on institutional investors. Since clients frequently replace the worst-performing managers (and since money managers live in fear of this), most managers try to avoid standing apart from the crowd. Those with only average results are considerably less likely to lose accounts than are the worst performers. The result is that most money managers consider mediocre performance acceptable. Although unconventional decisions that prove successful could generate superior investment performance and result in client additions, the risk of mistakes, which would diminish performance and possibly lead to client departures, is usually considered too high.

The Short-Term, Relative-Performance Derby

Like dogs chasing their own tails, most institutional investors have become locked into a short-term, relative-performance derby. Fund managers at one institution have suffered the distraction of hourly performance calculations; numerous managers are provided daily comparisons of their results with those of managers at other firms. Frequent comparative ranking can only reinforce a short-term investment perspective. It is understandably difficult to maintain a long-term view when, faced with the penalties for poor short-term performance, the long-term view may well be from the unemployment line.

The short-term orientation of money managers may be exacerbated by the increasing popularity of pension fund consultants. These consultants evaluate numerous money managers, compare their performances, contrast their investment styles, and then make recommendations to their clients. Because their recommendations can have a significant influence on the health of a money management business, the need to impress pension fund consultants may add to the short-term performance pressures on money managers.

What is a relative-performance orientation? Relative performance involves measuring investment results, not against an absolute standard, but against broad stock market indices, such as the Dow Jones Industrial Average or Standard & Poor's 500 Index, or against other investors' results. Most institutional investors measure their success or failure in terms of relative performance. Money managers motivated to outperform an index or a peer group of managers may lose sight of whether their investments are attractive or even sensible in an absolute sense.

Instead of basing investment decisions on independent and objective analysis, relative-performance-oriented investors really act as speculators. Rather than making sensible judgments about the attractiveness of specific stocks and bonds, they try to guess what others are going to do and then do it first. The problem is that even as one manager is attempting to guess what others may do, others are doing the same thing. The task becomes increasingly intricate: guess what the other guessers may guess. And so on.

Who is to blame for this short-term investment focus? Is it the fault of managers who believe clients want good short-term performance regardless of the level of risk or the impossibility of the task? Or is it the fault of clients who, in fact, do switch money managers with some frequency? There is ample blame for both to share.

There are no winners in the short-term, relative-performance derby. Attempting to outperform the market in the short run is futile since near-term stock and bond price fluctuations are random and because an extraordinary amount of energy and talent is already being applied to that objective. The effort only distracts a money manager from finding and acting on sound long-term opportunities as he or she channels resources into what is essentially an unwinnable game. As a result, the clients experience mediocre performance. The overall economy is also deprived, as funds are allocated to short-term trading rather than to long-term investments. Only brokers benefit from the high level of activity.

Other People's Money versus Your Own

You probably would not choose to dine at a restaurant whose chef always ate elsewhere. You should be no more satisfied with a money manager who does not eat his or her own cooking. It is worth noting that few institutional money managers invest their own money along with their clients' funds. The failure to do so frees these managers to singlemindedly pursue their firms', rather than their clients', best interests.

Economist Paul Rosenstein-Rodan has pointed to the "tremble factor" in understanding human motivation. "In the building practices of ancient Rome, when scaffolding was removed from a completed Roman arch, the Roman engineer stood beneath. If the arch came crashing down, he was the first to know. Thus his concern for the quality of the arch was intensely personal, and it is not surprising that so many Roman arches have survived."[3]

Why should investing be any different? Money managers who invested their own assets in parallel with clients would quickly abandon their relative-performance orientation. Intellectual honesty would be restored to the institutional investment process as the focus of professional investors would shift from trying to outguess others to maximizing returns under reasonable risk constraints. If more institutional investors strove to achieve good absolute rather than relative returns, the stock market would be less prone to overvaluation and market fads would less likely be carried to excess. Investments would only be made when they presented a compelling opportunity and not simply to keep up with the herd.

Impediments to Good Institutional Investment Performance

One major obstacle to good institutional investment performance is a shortage of time. There is more information available about securities, as well as corporate and macroeconomic developments, than anyone could reasonably digest. Just sifting through the accumulating piles of annual reports, Wall Street research, and financial periodicals could consume all of one's time every day. Thinking about and digesting all this material, of course, would take considerably longer.

An investor's time is required both to monitor current holdings and to investigate potential new investments. Since most money managers are always looking for additional assets to manage, however, they spend considerable time meeting with prospective clients in addition to hand-holding current clientele. It is ironic that all clients, present and potential, would probably be financially better off if none of them spent time with the money managers, but a free-rider problem exists in that each client feels justified in requesting periodic meetings. No single meeting places an intolerable burden on a money manager's time; cumulatively, however, the hours diverted to marketing can take a toll on investment results.

Another difficulty plaguing institutional investors is a bureaucratic decision-making process. While managing money successfully is not easy for anyone, many institutional investors compound that difficulty with a tendency toward conformity, inertia, and excessive diversification that results from group decision making.

Any institutional investor with an innovative or contrarian investment idea goes out on a limb. He or she assumes a personal risk within the firm, which compounds the investment risk. The cost of being wrong goes beyond the financial loss to include the adverse marketing implications as well as the personal career considerations. This helps explain why institutional investors rarely make unconventional investments. It also shows why they tend to hold onto fully priced or overpriced investments, unwilling to recommend sale unless a consensus for selling has already emerged. The multidimensional risk from holding too long is usually less than the risk in selling too soon.

Selling is difficult for money managers for three additional reasons. First, many investments are illiquid, and disposing of institutional-sized positions depends on more than simply the desire to do so. Second, selling creates additional work as sale proceeds must be reinvested in a subsequent purchase. Retaining current holdings is much easier. With so many demands on their time, money managers have little incentive to create additional work for themselves. Finally, the Securities and Exchange Commission (SEC), the governmental agency with regulatory responsibility for mutual funds, regards portfolio turnover unfavorably. Mutual fund managers thus have yet another reason to avoid selling.

Many large institutional investors separate analytical responsibilities from portfolio-management duties, with the portfolio managers senior to the analysts. The portfolio managers usually function on a top-down basis, integrating broad-scale market views with the analysts' recommendations to make particular investment decisions. This approach is conducive to mistakes since the people making the decisions have not personally analyzed the securities they are buying and selling. Moreover, the analysts who do have direct knowledge of the underlying companies may be swayed in their recommendations by any apparent top-down bias manifested by the portfolio managers.

There is one other impediment to good institutional investment performance: institutional portfolio managers are human beings. In addition to the influences of the investment business, money managers, despite being professionals, frequently fall victim to the same forces that operate on individual investors: the greedy search for quick and easy profits, the comfort of consensus, the fear of falling prices, and all the others. The twin burdens of institutional baggage and human emotion can be difficult to overcome.

Implications of Portfolio Size

Institutional investors are caught in a vicious circle. The more money they manage, the more they earn. However, there are

listed on an exchange, stocks and bonds of companies
cial distress or bankruptcy, and stocks not currently
dividend.

Fully Invested at All Times

ibility of institutional investors is frequently limited by
aposed requirement to be fully invested at all times.
stitutions interpret their task as stock picking, not mar-
ag; they believe that their clients have made the market-
lecision and pay them to fully invest all funds under
nagement.

ining fully invested at all times certainly simplifies the
ent task. The investor simply chooses the best available
ents. Relative attractiveness becomes the only invest-
rdstick; no absolute standard is to be met. Unfortunately
ortant criterion of investment merit is obscured or lost
abstandard investments are acquired solely to remain
rested. Such investments will at best generate mediocre
at worst they entail both a high opportunity cost—fore-
ne next good opportunity to invest—and the risk of
able loss.

ining fully invested at all times is consistent with a rela-
formance orientation. If one's goal is to beat the market
larly on a short-term basis) without falling significantly
it makes sense to remain 100 percent invested. Funds
ald otherwise be idle must be invested in the market in
at to underperform the market.

lute-performance-oriented investors, by contrast, will
y when investments meet absolute standards of value.
rill choose to be fully invested only when available
mities are both sufficient in number and compelling in
reness, preferring to remain less than fully invested
oth conditions are not met. In investing, there are times
ne best thing to do is nothing at all. Yet institutional
managers are unlikely to adopt this alternative unless
their competitors are similarly inclined.

diseconomies of scale in the returns e
large sums of money under management
dollar invested declines as total assets i
reason is that good investment ideas are i

Most of the major money manageme
large-capitalization securities for investn
cannot justify analyzing small and medi
which only modest amounts could ever b

To illustrate this point, consider a m
institution who oversees a $1 billion po
sonable but not excessive diversificati
have a policy of investing $50 million ir
ent stocks. To avoid owning illiquid
might be limited to no more than 5 per
shares of any one company. In combin
owning shares of companies with a mi
ization of $1 billion each (5 percent of $
At the beginning of 1991 there were or
market capitalizations this large, a fairly

I refer to this type of limitation on
behavior as a self-imposed constraint. T
a completely arbitrary rule adopted by r
portfolio dictates such a restriction. Unf
of large money managers, like the one
sands of companies are automatically
ment consideration regardless of indivic

Self-Imposed Constraints on In

Most institutional investors are limite
self-imposed constraints. In response t
dard and similar rules of acceptability
imposed restrictions on their portfolic
on the cash component of a portfol
investment in stocks selling below fiv

Overly Narrow Categorization

A common mistake institutional investors make is to allocate their assets into overly narrow categories. The portion of a port-folio that is targeted for equity investments, for example, cannot typically own bonds of bankrupt companies. Money assigned to junk-bond managers will be invested in junk bonds and noth-ing else, even when attractive opportunities are lacking. A municipal-bond portfolio will not usually be allowed to own taxable debt instruments. Such emphasis on rigidly defined cat-egories does not make sense. For example, a bond of a bankrupt company at the right price may have the risk and return charac-teristics of an equity investment. Equities such as utility stocks may demonstrate the stable cash-flow characteristics of high-quality bonds. Equity "stubs"—low-priced, highly leveraged stocks—may closely resemble warrants, offering high potential return but with considerable risk.

Allocating money into rigid categories simplifies investment decision making but only at the potential cost of lower returns. For one thing many attractive investments may lie outside tra-ditional categories. Also, the attractive historical returns that draw investors to a particular type of investment may have been achieved before the category was identified as such. By the time leveraged buyouts (LBOs) became a sought-after category of institutional investment, for example, the high returns avail-able from the early deals were no longer available.

Window Dressing

Window dressing is the practice of making a portfolio look good for quarterly reporting purposes. Some managers will deliberately buy shares of the current quarter's best market per-formers and sell shares of significant underperformers in order to dress up the portfolio's appearance in the quarterly report to clients. They also may sell positions with significant unrealized losses so that clients will not be reminded of major mistakes month after month. Such behavior is clearly uneconomic as well as intellectually insulting to clients; it also exacerbates price movements in either direction. Even so, as depressed issues drop further in price, attractive opportunities may be created for value investors.

Perhaps as a response to the difficulties of successfully managing institutional portfolios, a number of professional investors have abandoned fundamental analysis entirely. Rather than overcoming the problems of professional money management, however, they have compounded them. The remainder of this chapter describes their activities.

The Abandonment of Fundamental Investment Analysis by Institutional Investors

Over the past several years there has been an enormous increase in the amount of money managed by people who knowingly ignore the underlying fundamentals of the investments owned. Academic notions, such as the efficient-market hypothesis and the capital-asset-pricing model (three of whose most vociferous proponents received the Nobel Prize for economics in 1990), support these new investment strategies. Indexing is the primary investment outlet for investors who believe in these ideas. Practices such as tactical asset allocation, portfolio insurance, and program trading share to a greater or lesser extent the same disregard for investing based on company-by-company fundamentals.

Portfolio Insurance

Many institutional investors are forever seeking to uncover a magic formula for investment success. A successful formula would greatly simplify their lives; investing would become effortless, marketing would be a cinch, and they would almost immediately become extremely wealthy. The institutions persist in their search, but their mission is both ill-conceived and expensive for their client guinea pigs.

By way of example, in 1987 widespread popularity accrued to a technique that ostensibly allowed investors to truncate the downside risk of a portfolio of stocks in exchange for a slight reduction in potential return. This technique, cleverly labeled portfolio insurance, was hailed by Wall Streeters as a tool for risk reduction. It had the effect of encouraging institutional investors to buy stocks and remain fully invested despite the historically high market valuation that prevailed in the fall of 1987.

Portfolio insurance was, in fact, a simplistic notion dressed up in mathematical and computerized lingo. Simply put, the way portfolio insurance was supposed to work was that whenever the stock market declined by 3 percent, investors were to sell stock-index futures (a market basket of stocks to be delivered at a future date) to eliminate any further exposure to the market. In theory, then, the most that any investor could lose, no matter how much the market declined, was the first 3 percent. When prices staged a recovery, investors would repurchase the futures contracts and reestablish exposure to the market.

The obvious flaw is that past stock market fluctuations are not a useful guide to future performance. Just because the market declines 3 percent does not mean that it is about to drop further. If the market were to stage a sustained decline, investors would clearly benefit from eliminating market exposure. If a 3 percent decline were followed by a market recovery, however, investors would be forced to repurchase the futures and lock in a loss. In the event that market volatility is much greater than expected, the theory of portfolio insurance collapses, as repeated 3 percent losses are sustained.

Moreover, the market does not always rise and fall in an orderly fashion. There are days when the opening prices for many stocks are several points higher or lower than the previous day's close. When such a "gap" opening occurs, portfolio insurers might find it impossible to sell or repurchase futures as dictated by any formula.

As impractical as portfolio insurance is for any one investor, it becomes quite dangerous when large numbers of investors engage in it. With too many practitioners, frantic selling of stock index futures by portfolio insurers could drive futures prices below the underlying stock prices, making it profitable for arbitrageurs to buy the cheap futures and sell the underlying stocks. Such selling would put additional pressure on stock prices, perhaps necessitating more futures sales by portfolio insurers. A vicious circle could ensue.

This is exactly what happened on Monday, October 19, 1987. After a sharp market decline the previous week billions and billions of dollars' worth of stock index futures were dumped in relentless waves by portfolio insurers. This selling drove the futures as much as 10 percent below stock prices, creating an attractive opportunity for arbitrageurs to buy futures and sell stocks. This selling drove share prices even lower, triggering more sales of futures by hapless portfolio insurers. The notion that you could escape downside risk by selling futures was discredited in a couple of hours that day. Portfolio insurance had lured people who were not comfortable with the risks of stocks into buying and holding them. An apparently conservative strategy designed to prevent loss played an important role in the worst debacle in recent financial history.

Tactical Asset Allocation

By 1989, with portfolio insurance discredited, institutional investors returned to their computers searching for new formulas. Now their goal was to find a clear signal that would indicate whether stocks or bonds were the better buy. Although the search for this answer has preoccupied investors over the years, it is unlikely that a computer could ever be programmed to make what is clearly a judgment call. Yet what would have been considered a crackpot scheme if adopted by an individual investor became a popular institutional investment strategy known as tactical asset allocation.

Tactical asset allocation begins with a reasonable premise: there are times when bonds are a better buy than stocks and other times when the opposite holds true, and good investors should watch for opportunities to swap one for the other. Unfortunately the appropriate relationship between bond yields and stock prices cannot be incorporated into a computer program. There are simply too many variables to allow investors to determine a relationship today that will apply under every future scenario.

Another problem with tactical asset allocation is in its implementation. Neither the stock nor the bond market is infinitely deep. Vast sums cannot be instantaneously switched from one area to the other without moving the markets and incurring considerable transaction costs as well. Just because an asset allocation model dictates a portfolio decision does not mean that the implementation of that decision is feasible.

To illustrate this point, consider the actions of Renaissance Investment Management, Inc., on October 24, 1989. On that day Renaissance's computer decided to swing approximately $1 billion from U.S. Treasury bills into the stock market. Whether or not the computer conveyed good market timing, it had not been programmed to trade well. The computer instructed brokers to buy the designated stocks in such a way that the average purchase price for each security was below the day's closing price. It is not hard to imagine that a broker charged with such instructions would rush into the market late in the trading day, with the effect of making the closing price the day's high. The result of Renaissance's computer buy signal and the faulty instructions given to their brokers was a strong price run-up that day in virtually every one of the sixty stocks that Renaissance bought. According to *Barron's*, "Eleven of the twenty largest percentage gainers on the Big Board (NYSE) that day were Renaissance targets."[4] These stocks rose in price, not due to business fundamentals, but because the computer insisted on acquiring $1 billion worth of stocks by 4:00 p.m. on the day it gave its buy signal.

Index Funds: The Trend Toward Mindless Investing

An important stock market development in the past several years has been the rush by institutional investors into indexing. Indeed this trend may be a major factor in the significant divergence between the performances of large-capitalization and small-capitalization stocks between 1983 and 1990.

Indexing is the practice of buying all the components of a market index, such as the Standard & Poor's 500 Index, in proportion to the weightings of the index and then passively holding them. An index fund manager does not look to buy or sell even at attractive prices. Even more unusual, index fund managers may never have read the financial statements of the companies in which they invest and may not even know what businesses these companies are in.

Indexing has become increasingly popular among pension funds, endowments, and other long-term investment pools for several reasons. Indexing guarantees matching the performance of the securities in the index (although it also guarantees not outperforming it). Since the average institutional investor has underperformed the market for the past decade, and since all investors as a group must match the market because they collectively own the entire market, matching it may seem attractive. Indexing offers the additional benefits of very low transaction costs (as there is almost no trading) and low management fees (as the task requires virtually no thought or action).

Another reason for the trend toward indexing is that many institutional investors and pension funds believe in the efficient-market hypothesis. This theory holds that all information about securities is disseminated and becomes fully reflected in security prices instantaneously. It is therefore futile to try to out-perform the market. A corollary of this hypothesis is that there is no value to incremental investment research. The efficient-market theory can be expressed, according to Louis Lowenstein, "as a much-too-simplified thesis that one stock is as good as another and that, therefore, one might as well buy thousands of stocks as any one of them."[5]

By contrast, value investing is predicated on the belief that the financial markets are not efficient. Value investors believe that stock prices depart from underlying value and that investors can achieve above-market returns by buying under-valued securities. To value investors the concept of indexing is at best silly and at worst quite hazardous. Warren Buffett has observed that "in any sort of a contest—financial, mental or physical—it's an enormous advantage to have opponents who have been taught that it's useless to even try."[6] I believe that over time value investors will outperform the market and that choosing to match it is both lazy and shortsighted.

Indexing is a dangerously flawed strategy for several reasons. First, it becomes self-defeating when more and more investors adopt it. Although indexing is predicated on efficient markets, the higher the percentage of all investors who index, the more inefficient the markets become as fewer and fewer investors would be performing research and fundamental analysis. Indeed, at the extreme, if everyone practiced indexing, stock prices would never change relative to each other because no one would be left to move them.

Another problem arises when one or more index stocks must be replaced; this occurs when a member of an index goes bankrupt or is acquired in a takeover. Because indexers want to be fully invested in the securities that comprise the index at all times in order to match the performance of the index, the security that is added to the index as a replacement must immediately be purchased by hundreds or perhaps thousands of portfolio managers. There are implicit assumptions in indexing that securities markets are liquid, and that the actions of index-ers do not influence the prices of the securities in which they transact. Yet even very large capitalization stocks have limited liquidity at a given time. Owing to limited liquidity, on the day that a new stock is added to an index, it often jumps appreciably in price as indexers rush to buy. Nothing fundamental has changed; nothing makes that stock worth more today than yesterday. In effect, people are willing to pay more for that stock just because it has become part of an index.

By way of example, when Blockbuster Entertainment Corporation was added to the Standard and Poor's 500 Index in early 1991, its total market capitalization increased in one day by over $155 million, or 9.1 percent, because so many fund managers were "obliged" to buy it. Indeed, *Barron's* has calculated that stocks added to the Standard & Poor's 500 Index outperformed the market by almost 4 percent in the first week after their inclusion.[7]

A related problem exists when substantial funds are committed to or withdrawn from index funds specializing in small-capitalization stocks. (There are now a number of such funds.) Such stocks usually have only limited liquidity, and even a small amount of buying or selling activity can greatly influence the market price. When small-capitalization-stock indexers receive more funds, their buying will push prices higher; when they experience redemptions, their selling will force prices lower. By unavoidably buying high and selling low, small-stock indexers are almost certain to underperform their indexes.

Other perverse effects of indexing are now emerging with increasing frequency. When securities are owned only because they are part of an index and the only stated goal of the owners is to match the movements of that index, the portfolio "manager" responsible for those securities has virtually no interest in influencing the performance of the index. He or she is indifferent to whether the index rises or falls in value, other than to the extent that fees are based on total managed assets valued at market prices.

This means that in a proxy contest, it makes *no real difference* to the manager of an index fund whether the dissidents or the incumbent management wins the fight, even though the outcome may make a significant financial difference to the clients of the indexer. (By choosing indexing, investors have implicitly expressed the belief that their vote in a proxy contest could make no predictable financial difference anyway.) Ironically, even if indexers wanted to vote in a direction that maximized value, they would have absolutely no idea which way that would be because index fund managers typically have no fundamental investment knowledge about the stocks they own.[8]

It is noteworthy that the boom in indexing has occurred during a bull market. Between 1980 and 1990 the estimated amount of money managed in indexed accounts increased from $10 billion to about $170 billion, with 90 percent of that amount indexed to Standard & Poor's portfolios.[9] An additional $100 billion or more is believed to be "closet indexed," that is, to track, if not exactly match, the S&P 500 Index. According to *Barron's*, "No little impetus has been supplied to this melancholy trend by the harsh fact that the S&P has laid waste to the performance of conventional managers during the Eighties, particularly in the past five years. For example, the S&P has beaten the average equity mutual fund in the Lipper Analytical Service, Inc., survey in 24 out of the past 31 quarters."[10] The S&P 500 Index has also significantly bettered the broadly based Wilshire 5000 Index since the second half of 1983, outperforming it in twenty-three out of twenty-nine quarters; during that period the compound annual total return for the S&P 500 Index was 12.7 percent compared with 10.7 percent for the Wilshire 5000 Index.

I believe that indexing will turn out to be just another Wall Street fad. When it passes, the prices of securities included in popular indexes will almost certainly decline relative to those that have been excluded. More significantly, as *Barron's* has pointed out, "A self-reinforcing feedback loop has been created, where the success of indexing has bolstered the performance of the index itself, which, in turn promotes more indexing."[11] When the market trend reverses, matching the market will not seem so attractive, the selling will then adversely affect the performance of the indexers and further exacerbate the rush for the exits.

Conclusion

Investors must try to understand the institutional investment mentality for two reasons. First, institutions dominate financial-market trading; investors who are ignorant of institutional behavior are likely to be periodically trampled. Second, ample investment opportunities may exist in the securities that are excluded from consideration by most institutional investors. Picking through the crumbs left by the investment elephants can be rewarding.

Investing without understanding the behavior of institutional investors is like driving in a foreign land without a map. You may eventually get where you are going, but the trip will certainly take longer, and you risk getting lost along the way.

Notes

1. Louis Lowenstein, unpublished manuscript.
2. Louis Lowenstein, *What's Wrong with Wall Street* (Reading, Mass.: Addison-Wesley, 1988), p. 58.
3. John Silber, *Straight Shooting: What's Wrong with America and How To Fix It* (New York: Harper & Row, 1989), p. 163.
4. Jonathan R. Laing, "But Are They Heroes to Their Clients?" *Barron's* (30 October 1989): 11.
5. Lowenstein, *What's Wrong with Wall Street*, p. 3.
6. Berkshire Hathaway, Inc., annual report for 1988, p. 18.
7. Jonathan R. Laing, "Insidious Indexing," *Barron's* (15 January 1990): 8.
8. In addition to the impact on investors, this has frightening implications for economic efficiency in the United States.
9. Laing, "Insidious Indexing," p. 9.
10. Ibid., p. 8.
11. Ibid., p. 9.

4

Delusions of Value: The Myths and Misconceptions of Junk Bonds in the 1980s

The junk-bond boom would not have occurred without the enthusiastic acceptance of financial-market participants. The greed and possibly the ignorance of individual investors, the short-term orientation of institutional investors, and the tendency of Wall Street to maximize its self-interest above all came together in the 1980s to allow a $200 billion market to develop virtually from scratch. Although unproven over a complete economic cycle, newly issued junk bonds were hailed as a safe investment that provided a very attractive return to investors. By 1990, however, the concept of newly issued junk bonds had been exposed as seriously flawed, defaults reached record levels, and the prices of many issues plunged. Even so, the junk-bond market staged a surprising recovery in early 1991; many of the flaws that had resulted in tens of billions of dollars of losses were once again being ignored.

Historically many financial-market innovations have gained widespread acceptance before being exposed as ill conceived.

What is unique about junk bonds is the speed and magnitude of their rise; their strong and pernicious influence on other securities, on financial markets, and on the behavior of businesses; and their continued popularity in the face of large investor losses. Perhaps most important, junk bonds gave an upward propulsion to business valuation, as time-tested analytical standards and trusted yardsticks of value came to be either overlooked by investors or abandoned for new and unproven ones. This chapter is intended as a cautionary tale, an illustration of how seriously misguided investor thinking can become.

The junk-bond debacle was no great surprise. It had been predicted publicly by James Grant, editor of *Grant's Interest Rate Observer*, Louis Lowenstein, author of *What's Wrong with Wall Street*, Warren Buffett, chairman of Berkshire Hathaway, Inc., and me among others. The junk-bond market not only existed but actually thrived in the face of continued criticism and repeated warnings. The self-interest of the participants in its perpetuation was so great, however, that they used their collective influence to effectively stave off for a number of years the growing weight of evidence against junk bonds.

A Brief History of the Junk-Bond Market

To understand the junk-bond market and its amazing growth in the 1980s, one must begin with Michael Milken, its mastermind. In college and then at the University of Pennsylvania's Wharton School of Business in the early 1970s, Milken studied the work of academician W. Braddock Hickman. Two decades earlier Hickman had shown that a well-diversified, low-grade bond portfolio could earn a greater rate of return than a high-quality bond portfolio; in other words, the higher yields on low-rated securities would more than compensate for capital losses from any defaults.[1] This opportunity existed because risk-averse investors shunned low-grade bonds regardless of potential return. Hence such bonds traded at depressed prices, and low prices, not high coupons, were the driving force behind the attractive returns. As we shall see, the legitimate opportunity in a virtual handful of distressed securities that were overlooked by others was carried to excess when Milken extrapolated from a historical relationship to an entirely new type of security.

After graduating from the Wharton School, Milken took a job at Drexel Firestone, where he traded the bonds of "fallen angels," companies that had deteriorated in credit quality to below investment grade. According to legend, Milken commuted from his home outside Philadelphia to his Wall Street office by bus, spending the hours en route reading corporate financial statements by the dim light of a miner's headlamp that he wore. He soon became one of the most knowledgeable—and visible—people on Wall Street in the high-yield market.

The arguments in favor of high-yield-bond investing represented a radical departure from the conventional wisdom of the early 1980s. In the aftermath of the 1974-75 recession and bear market, investors were generally loathe to incur credit risk. Passage of the Employee Retirement Income and Security Act of 1974 (ERISA) led many institutions to adopt stringent fiduciary standards that precluded risk taking. Milken overcame investor reluctance by purportedly demonstrating that investment in low-rated securities historically provided higher total returns than could be earned on investment-grade securities.

The yield on low-rated bonds was obviously high. The new, radical claim was that the risk was also low: losses from defaults would be more than offset by incremental yield. This claim of a low default rate was central to the bullish case for junk bonds—a case that comes apart under even casual scrutiny.

Fallen-angel bonds typically are illiquid, and potential buyers are put off by the fear of being virtually locked into their investments. Another prerequisite to the establishment of a new-issue junk-bond market then was Milken's promise of liquidity. Milken promised buyers that he would make a market in all of his deals, ensuring liquidity. In the early days of the new-issue junk-bond market a great amount of paper was traded back and forth among a number of Milken disciples. This gave the appearance of liquidity, which was, in fact, only as deep as Milken's various pockets.

Before Michael Milken came along, the only junk bonds in existence were a few billion dollars' face amount of fallen angels. Investors were no more likely to buy newly issued junk bonds at par (the face value of a bond, the contractual amount of the bondholders' claim) than an offering of common stock in a bankrupt issuer. Milken shaped financial history by pioneering the issuance of junk bonds, glossing over the major differences between fallen angels and new issues. This required an enormous leap of faith, one which Milken made and was able to persuade others to make as well.

Unfortunately newly issued junk bonds were not the low-risk instruments that buyers were led to believe. They have, in fact, very different risk and return characteristics from fallen angels. Specifically, newly issued junk bonds offer no margin of safety to investors. Trading around par value, they have very limited appreciation potential, but unlike high-grade bonds trading near par, they have substantial downside risk. A fallen angel, by contrast, trades considerably below par and thus has less downside risk than newly issued junk bonds of comparable credit quality. The other side of this coin is that bonds trading below par have more upside price potential than bonds trading at par. If underlying credit quality improves or if interest rates drop, discount bonds have room for substantial appreciation; bonds trading at par, by contrast, are usually subject to call prior to maturity and thus have very limited upside potential. Other things being equal, then, newly issued junk bonds carry greater risk of loss with lower potential return than fallen angels, an important distinction that Milken failed to make, at least publicly.

The Flaws of the Default-Rate Calculation

There was, in fact, no reasonable basis for Milken's claim that the default rate of junk bonds issued in the late 1980s would be similar to the default rate of a small number of fallen angels issued at least a decade earlier. Yet this claim was a powerful selling tool for Milken's army of salespeople and an important factor in the widespread popularity that new-issue junk bonds came to achieve.

Of course, even the most overleveraged junk-bond issuers do not default immediately; it takes time to run short of cash. (A handful of issuers, such as Braniff, Inc., and Flight Transportation Corporation, managed to go bankrupt without making a single interest payment. Bonds such as theirs were referred to as NFCs [no first coupons].) For most of the 1980s the default-rate numerator (the volume of junk-bond defaults occurring in a given year) lagged behind the rapidly growing denominator (the total amount of junk bonds outstanding during that year). It was only when issuance virtually ceased in 1990 that the deterioration in credit quality was reflected in default-rate statistics.[2]

Meanwhile a number of other devices had been used by junk-bond underwriters to postpone the financial day of reckoning. One trick of the trade was to raise as much as 25-50 percent more cash than was immediately needed by issuers in order to fund upcoming cash-flow shortfalls. Needless to say, propping up marginal credits in this way helped maintain a low reported default rate, as it had when banks employed the device to put off defaults by their less-developed country (LDC) borrowers.

Widespread issuance of non-cash-pay (zero-coupon or pay-in-kind) securities also served to reduce the reported junk-bond default rate temporarily. The obvious reason is that non-cash-pay securities are less likely to default prior to maturity than cash-pay bonds since the absence of cash interest payment requirements eases the issuers' debt-service burden. Yet while such bonds allay the possibility of default for some issuers, they do not reduce it permanently. Indeed, such securities may be more likely than cash-pay securities to default ultimately because they accrue a growing debt burden that is not being serviced (and is often unserviceable) from current cash flows. The absence of default during a period when it is only being postponed is hardly a sign of fiscal health. An issuer of non-cash-pay junk bonds may actually be in trouble long before the actual event of default.

In the mid-1980s several academics produced studies concluding that junk bonds were attractive investments. In early 1990, even as the market was collapsing, Ed Altman edited *The High Yield Debt Market*, an anthology of more than a dozen recent articles mostly lauding junk-bond issuance and investment. Such upbeat analyses, sometimes financed by the leading high-yield underwriters, failed to take into account the serious flaws in the default-rate calculation.

The default rate was offered by underwriters, approved by academics, and accepted by investors as a proxy for investor losses from junk bonds that went bad. Not only was its calculation an exercise in science fiction, it also ignored the fact that defaults and investor losses are not the same thing. A fallen angel that defaults, for example, has not so far to drop as a junk bond trading at par. The default rate also failed to incorporate the financial impact of voluntary exchange offers and restructurings in which bondholders accepted impairment of their claims without an actual default having taken place.

The Junk-Bond Crusade

Junk bonds appeared to perform a sort of financial alchemy, as Louis Lowenstein has observed.[3] Owners of the junk bonds issued by the many companies whose interest expenses were greater than their pretax profits were able to claim to have earned interest income in excess of the profits earned by the underlying businesses. As long as investors were willing to purchase bonds on such terms, there were new underwritings to be done. And as long as the yield illusion was perpetuated, investors kept buying the bonds.

The tremendous growth of the market was accompanied by a buildup of the junk-bond infrastructure on Wall Street. If investors themselves failed to discern the attractiveness of junk bonds, Wall Street's analysts and salespeople would paint them a picture. By discarding old measurements of valuation and creating new ones and by mastering the art of optimistically projecting and compounding results further and further into the future, Wall Street was able to generate demand to match and at times even to exceed the burgeoning supply of junk bonds.

What had started as an attempt to generate fees and commissions from the sale of bonds began by the mid-1980s to take on the characteristics of a moral crusade. Investors wanted to believe that they could achieve returns much higher than ever before with no greater, and possibly even lower, risk. All the parties who stood to benefit from junk bonds—individual and institutional investors, underwriters, and brokers—"got religion," praying that junk bonds would turn out to be as miraculous as Milken preached. At the same time the sermon shifted from the low historical rate of default to a new theme: junk bonds as the economic salvation of America. Our country's nagging problems of slow growth, declining productivity, and diminished international competitiveness would quickly be solved through increased junk-bond issuance. The argument was that junk bonds could finance small, unknown companies that would not otherwise have been able to attract capital; such companies would innovate, grow, and create jobs, invest, and then grow some more. Although only a small proportion of all junk-bond issuers actually fit this description, and despite the obvious difficulty that such companies would have servicing large amounts of high-yield debt, these were the broad strokes painted by Milken, his colleagues, a number of academics, and many in the media.

At the same time that junk bonds were being portrayed as the friend of the small and otherwise unfinanceable business, they were also gaining stature as the enemy of the large and well-established corporation. Armed with billions of dollars in newly available cash, junk-bond-financed takeover artists and financial operators were suddenly in a position to buy almost any company in the country. To justify the use of junk bonds in corporate takeovers, large corporations were depicted as inefficient, administratively bloated, or even corrupt, and in desperate need of new managerial blood. While there were certainly kernels of truth in this characterization of corporate America, there was only scant consideration of whether the imposition of a staggering debt burden was the best remedy for this particular ailment. Moreover, virtually no one noticed or cared that junk bonds were no longer fulfilling their former, highly publicized role of financing small companies.

It seems incredible that anyone could get away with the portrayal of junk bonds as a kind of financial aspirin good for what ails you. Nevertheless, Milken had legions of loyal followers, many of whom he had helped make incredibly rich. Even the blue bloods of Wall Street like Morgan Stanley, First Boston, and Goldman Sachs, once threatened by Milken's burgeoning junk-bond empire, had by the mid-1980s built extensive junk-bond underwriting, marketing, and trading capabilities of their own. Albeit to a lesser degree than Milken, they too were now beneficiaries of the booming junk-bond market. The greatest irony in the whole junk-bond story may be that one of the biggest financial swindles of all time, newly issued junk bonds, had by the end of the 1980s come to enmesh every major Wall Street firm alongside Drexel Burnham Lambert. Long after the demise of Drexel, the rest of Wall Street would be licking its junk-bond-inflicted wounds, a nagging reminder of the widespread greed that wouldn't leave a shaky financial innovation to its power-hungry founder.

Early Successes of Junk-Bond Investors Led to Unrealistic Expectations

Self-fulfilling prophesies contributed to the successful junk-bond experiences of the early to mid-1980s. The increasing availability of nonrecourse junk-bond debt (in which the lender looks only to the borrowing entity for payment) led to increasing multiples being paid for corporate assets. This is because buyers armed with other people's money developed a skewed view of risk and return compared with that of buyers using their own money and were therefore willing to pay higher and higher prices. Business valuations started to increase at the same time; the economy was rebounding from the 1982 recession, and interest rates were falling from their early 1980s peak. Economic growth boosted operating results for many junk-bond issuers; declining interest rates allowed a number of issuers to refinance on advantageous terms. Even bad deals were bailed out by a growing economy and higher business valuations, reinforcing the notion of a low default rate. Early investors did well, emboldening others; subsequent deals were performed at still higher multiples of earnings and cash flow. Dr Pepper, Jack-in-the-Box, and Colt Industries, Inc., for example, were each bought and sold more than once at successively higher prices.

Most junk-bond buyers and issuers were probably unaware that they were implicitly assuming a great deal about the ongoing health of the economy and the junk-bond market. Many junk-bond issuers, for example, had razor-thin or nonexistent interest coverage (ratio of pretax earnings to interest expense) and insufficient cash flow to meet upcoming debt-principal repayments. Issuers and investors alike assumed that cash flow would always grow and that upcoming maturities could be refinanced. If growth did not materialize or if credit proved unavailable, a financial restructuring or bankruptcy filing would result. High-yield bonds were not purchased by cautious investors, however, but by optimistic, short-term-oriented, and gullible ones. It is not surprising that junk-bond holders did not expect an economic downturn or credit contraction; if they had, they would not have bought junk bonds.

The pervasive optimism of investors led to a relaxation of investment standards. A study by Barrie Wigmore, a limited partner at Goldman Sachs, showed that the typical interest coverage ratio for newly issued junk bonds declined drastically between 1980 and 1988 to the point where it fell below 1.0—that is, pretax earnings were less than interest expense for the average new junk issue. The ratio of debt to net tangible assets grew threefold over the same period to a level where issuers owed twice as much as the book value of their assets. In other words, regardless of any possible merits of earlier issues, the junk bonds of the late 1980s were bound to fail simply because the issuers were routinely overpaying for corporate assets.

The Major Buyers of Junk Bonds

High-Yield Bond Mutual Funds

Individual investors in the 1980s sought to preserve the high nominal returns to which they had recently become accustomed. These yield pigs were vulnerable to the hype that surrounded the junk-bond market, a vulnerability exacerbated by the favorable treatment given to high-yield bonds by the media. Many of these investors found their way into one of the many high-yield mutual funds that came into existence. These funds appeared to offer professional management, diversification, low transaction costs, and prudence, even as their prospectuses (assuming anyone read them) understated or even ignored the risks of junk-bond investment.

Competition among the mutual funds centered around the identity of the management company (e.g., Fidelity, T. Rowe Price) and the reported current yields to investors since assets tended to flow to the fund that reported the highest yield. Relative-performance-oriented fund managers therefore had a strong financial incentive to buy increasingly low-quality junk in order to enhance reported yields. "Gresham's Law of Junk Bonds" was at work: increasingly bad bonds drove out the good.

Mutual-fund managers are commonly subject to the constraint of being fully invested. The clients have made the asset-allocation decision, the thinking goes, and the job of fund managers is simply to put the money to work. Mutual funds thus occasionally purchased and held shaky junk bonds despite the better judgment of the portfolio managers themselves.

Thrifts

In the early 1980s deregulation enabled thrifts to expand into new and riskier areas of lending. Although the great majority of thrifts did not invest in junk bonds, a few dozen of them became big players.

Many justifications have been offered for investment by thrifts in junk bonds. In addition to the low-default-rate argument, proponents suggested that thrifts were better off investing in junk bonds, with their apparent marketability and low transaction costs, than in making direct loans to corporate borrowers, which require large and experienced lending staffs. Investing in junk bonds seemingly allowed small thrifts to effectively lend to much larger companies than they could reasonably have expected to do business with directly. The high yield on junk bonds also allowed thrift investors to significantly increase their interest rate spreads (the incremental yield on assets over the cost of liabilities) in the short run by incurring principal risk. Moreover, until late 1989 thrifts were not required to value their investment portfolios at market prices for accounting purposes; they could continue to report high net income regardless of large and growing unrealized losses on their junk-bond portfolios. Taking greater risk would, in the near-term, give thrifts the appearance of greater profitability and with it permit higher salaries to management and larger dividends to their owners.

Rationalizations aside, a single explanation for thrifts' investment in junk bonds stands out: owners and managers of thrifts had strong financial incentives to make these risky investments. Thrifts were able to attract deposits at relatively low cost. Since they were insured by the Federal Savings and Loan Insurance Corporation (FSLIC) up to $100,000 per account, most depositors did not need to look to the underlying creditworthiness of the institution or to its assets. They simply needed to consider the rate paid on deposits. In the presence of deposit insurance, the market could not and did not impose discipline on the investment behavior of thrift institutions. As long as junk bonds did not default in large numbers, the thrifts that invested in them would achieve high reported returns that belonged to the owners and to management. If the bonds defaulted, the FSLIC would bear the losses.

The largest thrift owners of junk bonds—Columbia Savings and Loan Association, CenTrust Savings and Loan Association, Imperial Savings and Loan Association, Lincoln Savings and Loan Association, and Far West Financial Corporation—were either insolvent or on the brink of insolvency by the end of 1990. Most of these institutions had grown rapidly through brokered deposits (deposits raised with the assistance of Wall Street) for the sole purpose of investing the proceeds in junk bonds and other risky assets. The legacy of thrift investment in junk bonds is that these investments caused major problems for institutions that otherwise would have been both considerably smaller and less troubled.

Insurance Companies

A number of insurance companies were also caught up in a cost-of-funds squeeze in the early 1980s. To investors seeking high yields they began to offer guaranteed investment contracts (GICs), whose attraction was the reinvestment of interest at contractual rates, effectively eliminating reinvestment risk.

When U.S. government bond yields were double digit, insurers were able to offer attractive rates on GICs while taking on little or no credit risk. When interest rates declined, insurers continued to offer high GIC yields in order to avoid a runoff of assets. To maintain a positive yield spread, insurance companies were forced to reach for yield, and many, like First Executive Corporation and First Capital Holdings Corporation, were lured into the junk-bond market. Unfortunately a number of their competitors felt compelled to bid for GIC business despite the risks of becoming junk-bond investors themselves. By 1990 a number of leading insurance companies had to take multimillion dollar writeoffs on their junk-bond investments, and First Executive and First Capital Holdings teetered on the edge of insolvency. In April 1991 state regulators seized First Executive's insolvent California and New York insurance subsidiaries as well as First Capital's California operations.

The Relaxation of Investment Standards

Junk-bond issuers, underwriters, and investors each abandoned established standards of value for new, less rigorous criteria. Excessive prices were paid for businesses by buyers able to issue risky paper to investors who in turn stretched their own customary analytical standards to justify the prices paid. New wrinkles, such as non-cash-pay bonds and interest rate reset features, camouflaged the relaxation of standards. The substitution of cash-flow analysis for other barometers of business performance also contributed. It is crucial that investors understand how the relaxation of standards came about, for the process was so subtle that many junk-bond buyers were probably not even aware that it had occurred.

Zero-Coupon and PIK Bonds Permit Financial Recklessness

Market receptiveness to nonrecourse zero-coupon and pay-in-kind (PIK) securities allowed takeover artists to engage in financial recklessness. Had the buyer of a highly leveraged business expected to pay cash interest from day one on the debt incurred in its purchase, his or her bid would have been modulated to chronologically match expected cash inflow with cash debt-service requirements. Zero-coupon and PIK debt, which accrue interest rather than paying it currently in cash, severed this tether of financial responsibility; bidders who are able to defer the financial day of reckoning far into the future are not constrained by financial reality. Nonrecourse zero-coupon and PIK junk-bond financing thus played a significant role in permitting historically unprecedented multiples to be paid for businesses in the mid-late 1980s.

Zero-coupon and PIK financing can act as corporate life support systems, preserving patients who are terminally ill. Such issuers can have liabilities that exceed assets and be unable to meet debt-service obligations in cash yet remain in business, giving an appearance of financial health. As Buffett has observed, "If LDC governments had issued no debt in the 1970s other than long-term zero-coupon obligations, they would now have a spotless record as debtors."[4]

Historically investors in bonds have enjoyed a presumption of solvency, safety, and even seniority. An investor in a U.S. Treasury bill, for example, or "zero-coupon U.S. government bond" (created synthetically when a Wall Street firm strips the cash flows from a U.S. Treasury bond and sells each payment serially) can be confident that income and principal will be paid at maturity. A junk zero-coupon bond, however, is a gamble; no cash is paid until maturity, at which point it either pays or defaults. Many buyers of zero-coupon or PIK junk bonds who believed that they were locking in an attractive yield to maturity turned out to have gambled and lost. Indeed, most junk zero-coupon and PIK instruments more closely resembled options on a future improvement in business results than fixed and secure claims against the current value of a company. Calling junk zero-coupon and PIK securities bonds didn't give them the same risk and return characteristics as other bonds, but it did make them easier to sell to investors.

Interest Rate Resets Work in Only One Direction

In the late 1980s interest rate resets became a common and widely accepted feature of newly issued junk bonds. An interest rate reset is a promise made by an issuer to adjust the coupon on a bond at a specified future date in order to cause it to trade at a predetermined price, usually par.[5] This reset feature, masquerading as a sort of financial guarantee, is really a financial placebo. It appears to provide a meaningful assurance of capital preservation but is virtually worthless. Created during an era when almost anyone could borrow a great deal of money, the misleading reset feature serves as a reminder that a promise is only as good as the entity that makes it.

For a bond reset to work properly, the underlying issuer must be creditworthy. Paradoxically, if the issuer is creditworthy, the reset feature is unnecessary (other than to adjust for appreciable interest rate movements in the economy or minor fluctuations in the issuer's creditworthiness). There is no interest rate, however, that will cause the bonds of a severely distressed issuer to trade at par; no matter how much the interest coupon is raised, the downside risk to prospective buyers holds down the bond's market price. Moreover, the higher the rate at which the coupon is reset, the worse off the issuer becomes, as increased debt-service requirements exacerbate the financial distress.

Numerous junk-bond resets failed in the late 1980s, and only a few succeeded. The bonds of Maxxam, Inc., were a near success; reset to trade at par, they failed to sell above 95, despite Maxxam's strong business results at the time. An issue of 16 percent Western Union Corporation bonds was reset to a 19.25 percent coupon at a time when Western Union already had one foot in the grave; the bond prices did not respond to the reset, declining quickly from the 80s to the 40s and then lower still. In 1989 Drexel Burnham Lambert was unable to reset the bonds of Jim Walter Corporation, which was then forced to file for bankruptcy.

In a daring display of financial chutzpah, Kohlberg, Kravis and Roberts (KKR), the buyer of RJR Nabisco, Inc. (RJR), in 1989, crammed down (distributed) $5 billion face value of reset-table PIK securities to former stockholders of that company as merger consideration. The perceived attractiveness of the reset feature may have allowed KKR's bid to prevail over competing offers, although the entire reset market was far less than the size of this issue alone and the record of previous reset attempts was abysmal. The reset feature, accepted by buyers as an almost ironclad guarantee, stirred enormous enthusiasm for the RJR cram-down paper. Some of the demand was from investors who didn't usually purchase junk bonds but were attracted by the apparent promise of "assured" par value.

The most widely quoted yield on the RJR Nabisco bonds and preferred stock was not the conventional current yield or yield to maturity but the newly coined "yield to reset." Substantial sums were invested based on this unproven concept, one that would work only if RJR Nabisco were financially healthy and if the junk-bond market were not in disarray. As it turned out, even after a last-ditch infusion of $1.5 billion of new equity capital into RJR Nabisco, the bonds failed to trade above 93 percent of par at the date of the reset. It was only later, after the company completed a more significant deleveraging, that the market price of the bonds reached par value.

An Analytical Error of Junk-Bond Investors

The relaxation of investment standards by junk-bond investors was accompanied by the dangerous misconception that the amount of debt and equity in a company's capital structure junior to one's own investment provided a degree of protection. It was as if the value of a business existed on the liability side rather than on the asset side of its balance sheet. Although it may be superficially reassuring to know that there are investors in a company whose claims are subordinated to your own, this information is of little, if any, value in assessing the merits of your investment.

At the time of the $25 billion RJR Nabisco leveraged buyout, Wall Street analysts argued that the issuance of $5 billion worth of cram-down debt and preferred stock improved the creditworthiness of RJR's senior debt. To illustrate the fallacy of this argument, suppose KKR had paid $129 rather than $109 per share for RJR in the form of an additional $4 billion of cramdown preferred stock. The senior lenders would have been no better off with this additional $4 billion of book equity junior to theirs. No more tangible assets would have belonged to the company than before; only the intangible asset called goodwill would have been increased via a bookkeeping entry. Moreover, the improved debt-to-equity ratio would have been irrelevant to the safety of the senior lenders. Emphasis on the junior claims against a company is a greater-fool argument, wherein one takes comfort from the potentially foolish actions of others rather than from the wisdom of one's own.

A Flawed Definition of Cash Flow, EBITDA, Leads to Overvaluation

Investors in public companies have historically evaluated them on reported earnings. By contrast, private buyers of entire companies have valued them on free cash flow. In the latter half of the 1980s entire businesses were bought and sold almost as readily as securities, and it was not unreasonable for investors in securities to start thinking more like buyers and sellers of entire businesses. There is, of course, nothing wrong with reexamining an old analytical tool for continued validity nor with replacing one that has become outmoded. Thus, in a radical departure from the historical norm, many stock and junk-bond buyers in the latter half of the 1980s replaced earnings with cash flow as the analytical measure of value.

In their haste to analyze free cash flow, investors in the 1980s sought a simple calculation, a single number, that would quantify a company's cash-generating ability. The cash-flow calculation the great majority of investors settled upon was EBITDA (earnings before interest, taxes, depreciation, and amortization). Virtually all analyses of highly leveraged firms relied on EBITDA as a principal determinant of value, sometimes as the only determinant. Even nonleveraged firms came to be analyzed in this way since virtually every company in the late 1980s was deemed a potential takeover candidate. Unfortunately EBITDA was analytically flawed and resulted in the chronic overvaluation of businesses.

How should cash flow be measured? Before the junk-bond era investors looked at two components: after-tax earnings, that is, the profit of a business; plus depreciation and amortization minus capital expenditures, that is, the net investment or disinvestment in the fixed assets of a business. The availability of large amounts of nonrecourse financing changed things. Since interest expense is tax deductible, pretax, not after-tax, earnings are available to pay interest on debt; money that would have gone to pay taxes goes instead to lenders. A highly leveraged company thus has more available cash flow than the same business utilizing less leverage.

Notwithstanding, EBIT (earnings before interest and taxes) is not necessarily all freely available cash. If interest expense consumes all of EBIT, no income taxes are owed. If interest expense is low, however, taxes consume an appreciable portion of EBIT. At the height of the junk-bond boom, companies could borrow an amount so great that all of EBIT (or more than all of EBIT) was frequently required for paying interest. In a less frothy lending environment companies cannot become so highly leveraged at will. EBIT is therefore not a reasonable approximation of cash flow for them. After-tax income plus that portion of EBIT going to pay interest expense is a company's true cash flow derived from the ongoing income stream.

Cash flow, as mentioned, also results from the excess of depreciation and amortization expenses over capital expenditures. It is important to understand why this is so. When a company buys a machine, it is required under generally accepted accounting principles (GAAP) to expense that machine over its useful life, a procedure known in accounting parlance as depreciation. Depreciation is a noncash expense that reduces net reported profits but not cash. Depreciation allowances contribute to cash but must eventually be used to fund capital expenditures that are necessary to replace worn-out plant and equipment. Capital expenditures are thus a direct offset to depreciation allowances; the former is as certain a use of cash as the latter is a source. The timing may differ: a company may invest heavily in plant and equipment at one point and afterward generate depreciation allowances well in excess of current capital spending. Whenever the plant and equipment need to be replaced, however, cash must be available. If capital spending is less than depreciation over a long period of time, a company is undergoing gradual liquidation.

Amortization of goodwill is also a noncash charge but, conversely, is more of an accounting fiction than a real business expense. When a company is purchased for more than its tangible book value, accounting rules require the buyer to create an intangible balance-sheet asset known as goodwill to make up for the difference, and then to amortize that goodwill over forty years. Amortization of goodwill is thus a charge that does not necessarily reflect a real decline in economic value and that likely need not be spent in the future to preserve the business. Charges for goodwill amortization usually do represent free cash flow.

It is not clear why investors suddenly came to accept EBITDA as a measure of corporate cash flow. EBIT did not accurately measure the cash flow from a company's ongoing income stream. Adding back 100 percent of depreciation and amortization to arrive at EBITDA rendered it even less meaningful. Those who used EBITDA as a cash-flow proxy, for example, either ignored capital expenditures or assumed that businesses would not make any, perhaps believing that plant and equipment do not wear out. In fact, many leveraged takeovers of the 1980s forecast steadily rising cash flows resulting partly from anticipated sharp reductions in capital expenditures. Yet the reality is that if adequate capital expenditures are not made, a corporation is extremely unlikely to enjoy a steadily increasing cash flow and will instead almost certainly face declining results.

It is not easy to determine the required level of capital expenditures for a given business. Businesses invest in physical plant and equipment for many reasons: to remain in business, to compete, to grow, and to diversify. Expenditures to stay in business and to compete are absolutely necessary. Capital expenditures required for growth are important but not usually essential, while expenditures made for diversification are often not necessary at all. Identifying the necessary expenditures requires intimate knowledge of a company, information typically available only to insiders. Since detailed capital-spending information was not readily available to investors, perhaps they simply chose to disregard it.

Some analysts and investors adopted the view that it was not necessary to subtract capital expenditures from EBITDA because *all* the capital expenditures of a business could be financed externally (through lease financing, equipment trusts, nonrecourse debt, etc.). One hundred percent of EBITDA would thus be free pretax cash flow available to service debt; no money would be required for reinvestment in the business. This view was flawed, of course. Leasehold improvements and parts of a machine are not typically financeable for any company. Companies experiencing financial distress, moreover, will have limited access to external financing for any purpose. An over-leveraged company that has spent its depreciation allowances on debt service may be unable to replace worn-out plant and equipment and eventually be forced into bankruptcy or liquidation.

EBITDA may have been used as a valuation tool because no other valuation method could have justified the high takeover prices prevalent at the time. This would be a clear case of circular reasoning. Without high-priced takeovers there were no up-front investment banking fees, no underwriting fees on new junk-bond issues, and no management fees on junk-bond port-folios. This would not be the first time on Wall Street that the means were adapted to justify an end. If a historically accepted investment yardstick proves to be overly restrictive, the path of least resistance is to invent a new standard.[6]

EBITDA Analysis Obscures the Difference between Good and Bad Businesses

EBITDA, in addition to being a flawed measure of cash flow, also masks the relative importance of the several components of corporate cash flow. Pretax earnings and depreciation allowance comprise a company's pretax cash flow; earnings are the return on the capital invested in a business, while depreciation is essentially a return *of* the capital invested in a business. To illustrate the confusion caused by EBITDA analysis, consider the example portrayed in exhibit 1.

Exhibit 1
Companies X and Y

Income Statement for 1990
($ in millions)

Service Company X		Manufacturing Company Y	
Revenue	$100	Revenue	$100
Cash Expenses	80	Cash Expenses	80
Depreciation and		Depreciation and	
Amortization	0	Amortization	20
EBIT	$ 20	EBIT	$ 0
EBITDA	$ 20	EBITDA	$ 20

Investors relying on EBITDA as their only analytical tool would value these two businesses equally. At equal prices, however, most investors would prefer to own Company X, which earns $20 million, rather than Company Y, which earns nothing. Although these businesses have identical EBITDA, they are clearly not equally valuable. Company X could be a service business that owns no depreciable assets. Company Y could be a manufacturing business in a competitive industry. Company Y must be prepared to reinvest its depreciation allowance (or possibly more, due to inflation) in order to replace its worn-out machinery. It has no free cash flow over time. Company X, by contrast, has no capital-spending requirements and thus has substantial cumulative free cash flow over time.

Anyone who purchased Company Y on a leveraged basis would be in trouble. To the extent that any of the annual $20 million in EBITDA were used to pay cash interest expense, there would be a shortage of funds for capital spending when plant and equipment needed to be replaced. Company Y would eventually go bankrupt, unable both to service its debt and maintain its business. Company X, by contrast, might be an attractive buyout candidate. The shift of investor focus from after-tax earnings to EBIT and then to EBITDA masked important differences between businesses, leading to losses for many investors.

Collateralized Junk-Bond Obligations

One of the last junk-bond-market innovations was the collateralized bond obligation (CBO). CBOs are diversified investment pools of junk bonds that issue their own securities with the underlying junk bonds as collateral. Several tranches of securities with different seniorities are usually created, each with risk and return characteristics that differ from those of the underlying junk bonds themselves.

What attracted underwriters as well as investors to junk-bond CBOs was that the rating agencies, in a very accommodating decision, gave the senior tranche, usually about 75 percent of the total issue, an investment-grade rating. This means that an issuer could assemble a portfolio of junk bonds yielding 14 percent and sell to investors a senior tranche of securities backed by those bonds at a yield of, say, 10 percent, with proceeds equal to perhaps 75 percent of the cost of the portfolio. The issuer could then sell riskier junior tranches by offering much higher yields to investors.

The existence of CBOs was predicated on the receipt of this investment-grade credit rating on the senior tranche. Greedy institutional buyers of the senior tranche earned a handful of basis points above the yield available on other investment-grade securities. As usual these yield pigs sacrificed credit quality for additional current return. The rating agencies performed studies showing that the investment-grade rating was warranted. Predictably these studies used a historical default-rate analysis and neglected to consider the implications of either a prolonged economic downturn or a credit crunch that might virtually eliminate refinancings. Under such circumstances, a great many junk bonds would default; even the senior tranche of a CBO could experience significant capital losses. In other words, a pile of junk is still junk no matter how you stack it.

Conclusion

Contrary to the promises of underwriters, junk bonds were a poor investment. They offered too little return for their substantial risk. To meet contractual interest and principal obligations, the number of things that needed to go right for issuers was high while the margin for error was low. Although the potential return was several hundred basis points annually in excess of U.S. Treasury securities, the risk involved the possible loss of one's entire investment.

Motivated by self-interest and greed, respectively, underwriters and buyers of junk bonds rationalized their actions. They accepted claims of a low default rate, and they used cash flow, as measured by EBITDA, as the principal determinant of underlying value. They even argued that a well-diversified portfolio of junk bonds was safe.

As this market collapsed in 1990, junk bonds were transformed into the financial equivalent of roach motels; investors could get in, but they couldn't get out. Bullish assumptions were replaced by bearish ones. Investor focus shifted from what might go right to what could go wrong, and prices plummeted.

Why should the history of the junk-bond market in the 1980s interest investors today? If you personally avoided investing in newly issued junk bonds, what difference should it make to you if other investors lost money? The answer is that junk bonds had a pernicious effect on other sectors of the financial markets and on the behavior of most financial-market participants. The overpricing of junk bonds allowed many takeovers to take place at inflated valuations. The excess profits enjoyed by the shareholders of the acquired companies were about equal to the losses eventually experienced by the buyers of this junk. Cash received by equity investors from junk-bond-financed acquisitions returned to the stock market, bidding up the prices of shares in still independent companies. The market prices of securities involved in arbitrage transactions, exchange offers, and corporate reorganizations were all influenced by the excessive valuations made possible by the junk-bond market. As a result, even those who avoided owning junk bonds found it difficult to escape their influence completely.

We may confidently expect that there will be new investment fads in the future. They too will expand beyond the rational limitations of the innovation. As surely as this will happen, it is equally certain that no bells will toll to announce the excess. Investors who study the junk-bond debacle may be able to identify these new fads for what they are and avoid them. And as we shall see in the chapters that follow, avoiding losses is the most important prerequisite to investment success.

Notes

1. Connie Bruck, *The Predators' Ball* (New York: Penguin, 1989), p. 28.
2. A more appropriate method would have been to examine defaults or, better still, total investment returns for junk bonds grouped by year of issuance, which would have eliminated the arithmetic flaws in the customary default-rate calculation.
3. Louis Lowenstein, "Lessons for Wall Street from Main Street," *Columbia Magazine* (October 1989): 26–27.
4. Berkshire Hathaway, Inc., annual report for 1989, p. 19.
5. Par is usually $1,000, but bond prices are expressed as percentages of par; a bond trading at 90 is worth 90 percent of its $1,000 par value, or $900.
6. Analysts frequently compounded the error of using EBITDA as a proxy for free cash flow by comparing it with cash interest expense rather than with total interest expense in determining the cash flow coverage of interest. The ratio of the cash generated if a business fails to reinvest, to only the interest that it must have pay currently, is not only meaningless; it smacks of deliberate deception.

II
A VALUE-INVESTMENT PHILOSOPHY

5

Defining Your Investment Goals

Warren Buffett likes to say that the first rule of investing is "Don't lose money," and the second rule is, "Never forget the first rule." I too believe that avoiding loss should be the primary goal of every investor. This does not mean that investors should never incur the risk of any loss at all. Rather "don't lose money" means that over several years an investment portfolio should not be exposed to appreciable loss of principal.

While no one wishes to incur losses, you couldn't prove it from an examination of the behavior of most investors and speculators. The speculative urge that lies within most of us is strong; the prospect of a free lunch can be compelling, especially when others have already seemingly partaken. It can be hard to concentrate on potential losses while others are greedily reaching for gains and your broker is on the phone offering shares in the latest "hot" initial public offering. Yet the avoidance of loss is the surest way to ensure a profitable outcome.

A loss-avoidance strategy is at odds with recent conventional market wisdom. Today many people believe that risk comes, not from owning stocks, but from not owning them. Stocks as a group, this line of thinking goes, will outperform bonds or cash equivalents over time, just as they have in the past. Indexing is one manifestation of this view. The tendency of most institutional investors to be fully invested at all times is another.

There is an element of truth to this notion; stocks do figure to outperform bonds and cash over the years. Being junior in a company's capital structure and lacking contractual cash flows and maturity dates, equities are inherently riskier than debt instruments. In a corporate liquidation, for example, the equity only receives the residual after all liabilities are satisfied. To persuade investors to venture into equities rather than safer debt instruments, they must be enticed by the prospect of higher returns. However, as discussed at greater length in chapter 7, the actual risk of a particular investment cannot be determined from historical data. It depends on the price paid. If enough investors believe the argument that equities will offer the best long-term returns, they may pour money into stocks, bidding prices up to levels at which they no longer offer the superior returns. The risk of loss stemming from equity's place in the capital structure is exacerbated by paying a higher price.

Another common belief is that risk avoidance is incompatible with investment success. This view holds that high return is attainable only by incurring high risk and that long-term investment success is attainable only by seeking out and bearing, rather than avoiding, risk. Why do I believe, conversely, that risk avoidance is the single most important element of an investment program? If you had $1,000, would you be willing to wager it, double or nothing, on a fair coin toss? Probably not. Would you risk your entire net worth on such a gamble? Of course not. Would you risk the loss of, say, 30 percent of your net worth for an equivalent gain? Not many people would because the loss of a substantial amount of money could impair their standard of living while a comparable gain might not improve it commensurately. If you are one of the vast majority of investors who are risk averse, then loss avoidance must be the cornerstone of your investment philosophy.

Greedy, short-term-oriented investors may lose sight of a sound mathematical reason for avoiding loss: the effects of compounding even moderate returns over many years are compelling, if not downright mind boggling. Table 1 shows the delightful effects of compounding even relatively small amounts.

Table 1

Compound Value of $1,000 Invested at Different Rates of Return
and for Varying Durations

Rate	5 years	10 years	20 years	30 years
6%	$ 1,338	$ 1,791	$ 3,207	$ 5,743
8%	1,469	2,159	4,661	10,063
10%	1,611	2,594	6,727	17,449
12%	1,762	3,106	9,646	29,960
16%	2,100	4,411	19,461	85,850
20%	2,488	6,192	38,338	237,376

As the table illustrates, perseverance at even relatively modest rates of return is of the utmost importance in compounding your net worth. A corollary to the importance of compounding is that it is very difficult to recover from even one large loss, which could literally destroy all at once the beneficial effects of many years of investment success. In other words, an investor is more likely to do well by achieving consistently good returns with limited downside risk than by achieving volatile and sometimes even spectacular gains but with considerable risk of principal. An investor who earns 16 percent annual returns over a decade, for example, will, perhaps surprisingly, end up with more money than an investor who earns 20 percent a year for nine years and then loses 15 percent the tenth year.

There is an understandable, albeit uneconomic, appeal to the latter pattern of returns, however. The second investor will outperform the former nine years out of ten, gaining considerable psychic income from this apparently superior performance. If both investors are money management professionals, the latter may also have a happier clientele (90 percent of the time, they will be doing better) and thus a more successful company. This may help to explain why risk avoidance is not the primary focus of most institutional investors.

One of the recurrent themes of this book is that the future is unpredictable. No one knows whether the economy will shrink or grow (or how fast), what the rate of inflation will be, and whether interest rates and share prices will rise or fall. Investors intent on avoiding loss consequently must position themselves to survive and even prosper under any circumstances. Bad luck can befall you; mistakes happen. The river may overflow its banks only once or twice in a century, but you still buy flood insurance on your house each year. Similarly we may only have one or two economic depressions or financial panics in a century and hyperinflation may never ruin the U.S. economy, but the prudent, farsighted investor manages his or her portfolio with the knowledge that financial catastrophes can and do occur. Investors must be willing to forego some near-term return, if necessary, as an insurance premium against unexpected and unpredictable adversity.

Choosing to avoid loss is not a complete investment strategy; it says nothing about what to buy and sell, about which risks are acceptable and which are not. A loss-avoidance strategy does not mean that investors should hold all or even half of their portfolios in U.S. Treasury bills or own sizable caches of gold bullion. Rather, investors must be aware that the world can change unexpectedly and sometimes dramatically; the future may be very different from the present or recent past. Investors must be prepared for any eventuality.

Many investors mistakenly establish an investment goal of achieving a specific rate of return. Setting a goal, unfortunately, does not make that return achievable. Indeed, no matter what the goal, it may be out of reach. Stating that you want to earn, say, 15 percent a year, does not tell you a thing about how to achieve it. Investment returns are not a direct function of how long or hard you work or how much you wish to earn. A ditch digger can work an hour of overtime for extra pay, and a piece worker earns more the more he or she produces. An investor cannot decide to think harder or put in overtime in order to achieve a higher return. All an investor can do is follow a consistently disciplined and rigorous approach; over time the returns will come.

Targeting investment returns leads investors to focus on upside potential rather than on downside risk. Depending on the level of security prices, investors may have to incur considerable downside risk to have a chance of meeting predetermined return objectives. If Treasury bills yield 6 percent, more cannot be achieved from owning them. If thirty-year government bonds yield 8 percent, it is possible, for a while, to achieve a 15 percent annual return through capital appreciation resulting from a decline in interest rates. If the bonds are held to maturity, however, the return will be 8 percent.

Stocks do not have the firm mathematical tether afforded by the contractual nature of the cash flows of a high-grade bond. Stocks, for example, have no maturity date or price. Moreover, while the value of a stock is ultimately tied to the performance of the underlying business, the potential profit from owning a stock is much more ambiguous. Specifically, the owner of a stock does not receive the cash flows from a business; he or she profits from appreciation in the share price, presumably as the market incorporates fundamental business developments into that price. Investors thus tend to predict their returns from investing in equities by predicting future stock prices. Since stock prices do not appreciate in a predictable fashion but fluctuate unevenly over time, almost any forecast can be made and justified. It is thus possible to predict the achievement of any desired level of return simply by fiddling with one's estimate of future share prices.

In the long run, however, stock prices are also tethered, albeit more loosely than bonds, to the performance of the underlying businesses. If the prevailing stock price is not warranted by underlying value, it will eventually fall. Those who bought in at a price that itself reflected overly optimistic assumptions will incur losses.

Rather than targeting a desired rate of return, even an eminently reasonable one, investors should target risk. Treasury bills are the closest thing to a riskless investment; hence the interest rate on Treasury bills is considered the risk-free rate. Since investors always have the option of holding all of their money in T-bills, investments that involve risk should only be made if they hold the promise of considerably higher returns than those available without risk. This does not express an investment preference for T-bills; to the contrary, you would rather be fully invested in superior alternatives. But alternatives with some risk attached are superior only if the return more than fully compensates for the risk.

Most investment approaches do not focus on loss avoidance or on an assessment of the real risks of an investment compared with its return. Only one that I know does: value investing. Chapter 6 describes value investing; chapter 7 elaborates on three of its central underpinnings. Both chapters expand on the theme of loss avoidance and consider various means of achieving this objective.

6

Value Investing: The Importance of a Margin of Safety

Value investing is the discipline of buying securities at a significant discount from their current underlying values and holding them until more of their value is realized. The element of a bargain is the key to the process. In the language of value investors, this is referred to as buying a dollar for fifty cents. Value investing combines the conservative analysis of underlying value with the requisite discipline and patience to buy only when a sufficient discount from that value is available. The number of available bargains varies, and the gap between the price and value of any given security can be very narrow or extremely wide. Sometimes a value investor will review in depth a great many potential investments without finding a single one that is sufficiently attractive. Such persistence is necessary, however, since value is often well hidden.

The disciplined pursuit of bargains makes value investing very much a risk-averse approach. The greatest challenge for value investors is maintaining the required discipline. Being a value investor usually means standing apart from the crowd, challenging conventional wisdom, and opposing the prevailing investment winds. It can be a very lonely undertaking. A value investor may experience poor, even horrendous, performance compared with that of other investors or the market as a whole during prolonged periods of market overvaluation. Yet over the long run the value approach works so successfully that few, if any, advocates of the philosophy ever abandon it.

Waiting for the Right Pitch

Warren Buffett uses a baseball analogy to articulate the discipline of value investors. A long-term-oriented value investor is a batter in a game where no balls or strikes are called, allowing dozens, even hundreds, of pitches to go by, including many at which other batters would swing. Value investors are students of the game; they learn from every pitch, those at which they swing and those they let pass by. They are not influenced by the way others are performing; they are motivated only by their own results. They have infinite patience and are willing to wait until they are thrown a pitch they can handle—an undervalued investment opportunity.

Value investors will not invest in businesses that they cannot readily understand or ones they find excessively risky. Hence few value investors will own the shares of technology companies. Many also shun commercial banks, which they consider to have unanalyzable assets, as well as property and casualty insurance companies, which have both unanalyzable assets and liabilities.

Most institutional investors, unlike value investors, feel compelled to be fully invested at all times. They act as if an umpire were calling balls and strikes—mostly strikes—thereby forcing them to swing at almost every pitch and forego batting selectivity for frequency. Many individual investors, like amateur ballplayers, simply can't distinguish a good pitch from a wild one. Both undiscriminating individuals and constrained institutional investors can take solace from knowing that most market participants feel compelled to swing just as frequently as they do.

For a value investor a pitch must not only be in the strike zone, it must be in his "sweet spot." Results will be best when the investor is not pressured to invest prematurely. There may be times when the investor does not lift the bat from his shoulder; the cheapest security in an overvalued market may still be overvalued. You wouldn't want to settle for an investment offering a safe 10 percent return if you thought it very likely that another offering an equally safe 15 percent return would soon materialize.

An investment *must* be purchased at a discount from underlying worth. This makes it a good absolute value. Being a good absolute value alone, however, is not sufficient for investors must choose only the best absolute values among those that are currently available. A stock trading at one-half of its underlying value may be attractive, but another trading at one-fourth of its worth is the better bargain. This dual discipline compounds the difficulty of the investment task for value investors compared with most others.

Value investors continually compare potential new investments with their current holdings in order to ensure that they own only the most undervalued opportunities available. Investors should never be afraid to reexamine current holdings as new opportunities appear, even if that means realizing losses on the sale of current holdings. In other words, no investment should be considered sacred when a better one comes along.

Sometimes dozens of good pitches are thrown consecutively to a value investor. In panicky markets, for example, the number of undervalued securities increases and the degree of undervaluation also grows. In buoyant markets, by contrast, both the number of undervalued securities and their degree of undervaluation declines. When attractive opportunities are plentiful, value investors are able to sift carefully through all the bargains for the ones they find most attractive. When attractive opportunities are scarce, however, investors must exhibit great self-discipline in order to maintain the integrity of the valuation process and limit the price paid. Above all, investors must always avoid swinging at bad pitches.

The Complexity and Variability of Business Valuation

It would be a serious mistake to think that all the facts that describe a particular investment are or could be known. Not only may questions remain unanswered; all the right questions may not even have been asked. Even if the present could somehow be perfectly understood, most investments are dependent on outcomes that cannot be accurately foreseen.

Even if everything could be known about an investment, the complicating reality is that business values are not carved in stone. Investing would be much simpler if business values did remain constant while stock prices revolved predictably around them like the planets around the sun. If you cannot be certain of value, after all, then how can you be certain that you are buying at a discount? The truth is that you cannot.

There are many explanations for volatility in business value. The "credit cycle," the periodic tightening and relaxation of the availability of credit, is a major factor, for example, because it influences the cost and terms upon which money can be borrowed. This in turn affects the multiples that buyers are willing to pay for businesses. Simply put, buyers will willingly pay higher multiples if they receive low-rate nonrecourse financing than they will in an unleveraged transaction.

Trends in inflation or deflation also cause business values to fluctuate. That said, value investing can work very well in an inflationary environment. If for fifty cents you buy a dollar of value in the form of an asset, such as natural resource properties or real estate, which increases in value with inflation, a fifty-cent investment today can result in the realization of value appreciably greater than one dollar. In an inflationary environment, however, investors may become somewhat careless. As long as assets are rising in value, it would appear attractive to relax one's standards and purchase $1 of assets, not for 50 cents, but for 70 or 80 cents (or perhaps even $1.10). Such laxity could prove costly, however, in the event that inflation comes to be anticipated by most investors, who respond by bidding up security prices. A subsequent slowdown in the rate of inflation could cause a price decline.

In a deflationary environment assets tend to decline in value. Buying a dollar's worth of assets for fifty cents may not be a bargain if the asset value is dropping. Historically investors have found attractive opportunities in companies with substantial "hidden assets," such as an overfunded pension fund, real estate carried on the balance sheet below market value, or a profitable finance subsidiary that could be sold at a significant gain. Amidst a broad-based decline in business and asset values, however, some hidden assets become less valuable and in some cases may become hidden liabilities. A decline in the stock market will reduce the value of pension fund assets; previously overfunded plans may become underfunded. Real estate, carried on companies' balance sheets at historical cost, may no longer be undervalued. Overlooked subsidiaries that were once hidden jewels may lose their luster.

The possibility of sustained decreases in business value is a dagger at the heart of value investing (and is not a barrel of laughs for other investment approaches either). Value investors place great faith in the principle of assessing value and then buying at a discount. If value is subject to considerable erosion, then how large a discount is sufficient?

Should investors worry about the possibility that business value may decline? Absolutely. Should they do anything about it? There are three responses that might be effective. First, since investors cannot predict when values will rise or fall, valuation should always be performed conservatively, giving considerable weight to worst-case liquidation value as well as to other methods. Second, investors fearing deflation could demand a greater than usual discount between price and underlying value in order to make new investments or to hold current positions. This means that normally selective investors would probably let even more pitches than usual go by. Finally, the prospect of asset deflation places a heightened importance on the time frame of investments and on the presence of a catalyst for the realization of underlying value. In a deflationary environment, if you cannot tell whether or when you will realize underlying value, you may not want to get involved at all. If underlying value is realized in the near-term directly for the benefit of shareholders, however, the longer-term forces that could cause value to diminish become moot.

The Importance of a Margin of Safety

Benjamin Graham understood that an asset or business worth $1 today could be worth 75 cents or $1.25 in the near future. He also understood that he might even be wrong about today's value. Therefore Graham had no interest in paying $1 for $1 of value. There was no advantage in doing so, and losses could result. Graham was only interested in buying at a substantial discount from underlying value. By investing at a discount, he knew that he was unlikely to experience losses. The discount provided a margin of safety.

Because investing is as much an art as a science, investors need a margin of safety. A margin of safety is achieved when securities are purchased at prices sufficiently below underlying value to allow for human error, bad luck, or extreme volatility in a complex, unpredictable, and rapidly changing world. According to Graham, "The margin of safety is always dependent on the price paid. For any security, it will be large at one price, small at some higher price, nonexistent at some still higher price."[1]

Buffett described the margin of safety concept in terms of tolerances: "When you build a bridge, you insist it can carry 30,000 pounds, but you only drive 10,000-pound trucks across it. And that same principle works in investing."[2]

What is the requisite margin of safety for an investor? The answer can vary from one investor to the next. How much bad luck are you willing and able to tolerate? How much volatility in business values can you absorb? What is your tolerance for error? It comes down to how much you can afford to lose.

Most investors do not seek a margin of safety in their holdings. Institutional investors who buy stocks as pieces of paper to be traded and who remain fully invested at all times fail to achieve a margin of safety. Greedy individual investors who follow market trends and fads are in the same boat. The only margin investors who purchase Wall Street underwritings or financial-market innovations usually experience is a margin of peril.

Even among value investors there is ongoing disagreement concerning the appropriate margin of safety. Some highly successful investors, including Buffett, have come increasingly to recognize the value of intangible assets—broadcast licenses or soft-drink formulas, for example—which have a history of growing in value without any investment being required to maintain them. Virtually all cash flow generated is free cash flow.

The problem with intangible assets, I believe, is that they hold little or no margin of safety. The most valuable assets of Dr Pepper/Seven-Up, Inc., by way of example, are the formulas that give those soft drinks their distinctive flavors. It is these intangible assets that cause Dr Pepper/Seven-Up, Inc., to be valued at a high multiple of tangible book value. If something goes wrong—tastes change or a competitor makes inroads—the margin of safety is quite low.

Tangible assets, by contrast, are more precisely valued and therefore provide investors with greater protection from loss. Tangible assets usually have value in alternate uses, thereby providing a margin of safety. If a chain of retail stores becomes unprofitable, for example, the inventories can be liquidated, receivables collected, leases transferred, and real estate sold. If consumers lose their taste for Dr Pepper, by contrast, tangible assets will not meaningfully cushion investors' losses.

How can investors be certain of achieving a margin of safety? By always buying at a significant discount to underlying business value and giving preference to tangible assets over intangibles. (This does not mean that there are not excellent investment opportunities in businesses with valuable intangible assets.) By replacing current holdings as better bargains come along. By selling when the market price of any investment comes to reflect its underlying value and by holding cash, if necessary, until other attractive investments become available.

Investors should pay attention not only to *whether* but also to *why* current holdings are undervalued. It is critical to know why you have made an investment and to sell when the reason for owning it no longer applies. Look for investments with catalysts that may assist directly in the realization of underlying value. Give preference to companies having good managements with a personal financial stake in the business. Finally, diversify your holdings and hedge when it is financially attractive to do so. Each of these points is discussed in the chapters comprising the remainder of this book.

To appreciate the margin of safety concept, consider the stock of Erie Lackawanna, Inc., in late 1987, when it was backed by nearly $140 per share in cash as well as a sizable and well-supported tax refund claim against the IRS. The stock sold at prices as low as $110 per share, a discount from the net cash per share even exclusive of the refund claim. The downside risk appeared to be zero. The only foreseeable loss on the stock would be a temporary market-price decline, a development that would merely render the shares a still better buy. Ultimately Erie Lackawanna won its tax case. Through mid-1991 cumulative liquidating distributions of $179 per share had been paid ($115 was paid in 1988, returning all of a buyer's late 1987 cost), and the stock still traded at approximately $8 per share.

Similarly Public Service Company of New Hampshire (PSNH) 18 percent second-mortgage bonds traded in early 1989 at about par value. Although formally in bankruptcy PSNH had continued to pay current interest on these bonds because their principal amount was covered many times over by the value of the utility assets securing them. The contractual maturity date of these bonds was June 1989, but investors were uncertain whether or not they would be retired if the company were then still in Chapter 11. Other than the possibility of a near-doubling of interest rates, there was immaterial downside risk other than from short-term price fluctuations. PSNH ultimately raised money to retire the bonds in November 1989, several months after their contractual maturity date. Investors were able to earn annualized returns of 18 percent with very low risk due to the uncertain timing of the bonds' redemption.

Perhaps the best recent example of investing with a margin of safety occurred in the debt securities of Texaco, Inc. In 1987 Texaco filed for bankruptcy as a result of uncertainty surrounding a $10 billion legal verdict against it in favor of Pennzoil. Although the value of Texaco's assets appeared to more than fully cover all of its liabilities even under a worst-case scenario, in the immediate aftermath of Texaco's Chapter 11 filing its stock and bonds plunged in price. As with any bankruptcy, many investors were suddenly constrained from owning Texaco securities. Even the company's public statement that bondholders would receive all principal and postpetition as well as prepetition interest failed to boost prices much.

The specific opportunity in Texaco securities was exemplified by the Texaco 11.875 percent debentures due May 1, 1994. These bonds traded actively at the 90 level (they traded flat; the price incorporated approximately eighteen months of accrued interest) in the wake of the October 1987 stock market crash. Assuming the full payment of principal and interest upon emergence from Chapter 11, these bonds purchased at 90 would provide annualized returns of 44.1 percent, 25.4 percent, and 19.5 percent, respectively, assuming a one-year, two-year, and three-year holding period from November 1, 1987. Could these bonds have declined further in price? Certainly, but they would simply have become a better buy. Uncertainty regarding the timing and exact resolution of the bankruptcy created an outstanding opportunity for value investors who were content with doing well under any scenario while always having a considerable margin of safety.

Value Investing Shines in a Declining Market

When the overall market is strong, the rising tide lifts most ships. Profitable investments are easy to come by, mistakes are not costly, and high risks seem to pay off, making them seem reasonable in retrospect. As the saying goes, "You can't tell who's swimming naked till the tide goes out."

A market downturn is the true test of an investment philosophy. Securities that have performed well in a strong market are usually those for which investors have had the highest expectations. When these expectations are not realized, the securities, which typically have no margin of safety, can plummet. Stocks that fit this description are sometimes referred to as "torpedo stocks," a term that describes the disastrous effect owning them can have on one's investment results. Compaq Computer Corporation traded at 72 on March 6, 1991. By April 24 the shares had fallen to 61⅞. The next day they plunged 9⅜ points. Then on May 14 they plunged 13¼ points to close at 36. The March 6 share price had reflected investor expectations of high earnings growth. When the company subsequently announced a decline in first-quarter earnings, the stock was torpedoed.

The securities owned by value investors are not buoyed by such high expectations. To the contrary, they are usually unheralded or just ignored. In depressed financial markets, it is said, some securities are so out of favor that you cannot give them away. Some stocks sell below net working capital per share, and a few sell at less than net cash (cash on hand less all debt) per share; many stocks trade at an unusually low multiple of current earnings and cash flow and at a significant discount to book value.

A notable feature of value investing is its strong performance in periods of overall market decline. Whenever the financial markets fail to fully incorporate fundamental values into securities prices, an investor's margin of safety is high. Stock and bond prices may anticipate continued poor business results, yet securities priced to reflect those depressed fundamentals may have little room to fall further. Moreover, securities priced as if nothing could go right stand to benefit from a change in perception. If investors refocused on the strengths rather than on the difficulties, higher security prices would result. When fundamentals do improve, investors could benefit both from better results and from an increased multiple applied to them.

In early 1987 the shares of Telefonos de Mexico, S.A., sold for prices as low as ten cents. The company was not doing badly, and analysts were forecasting for the shares annual earnings of fifteen cents and a book value of approximately seventy-five cents in 1988. Investors seemed to focus only on the continual dilution of the stock, stemming from quarterly 6.25 percent stock dividends and from the issuance of shares to new telephone subscribers, ostensibly to fund the required capital outlays to install their phones. The market ignored virtually every criterion of value, pricing the shares at extremely low multiples of earnings and cash flow while completely disregarding book value.

In early 1991 Telefonos's share price rose to over $3.25. The shares, out of favor several years earlier, became an institutional favorite. True, some improvement in operating results did contribute to this enormous price appreciation, but the primary explanation was an increase in the multiple investors were willing to pay. The higher multiple reflected a change in investor psychology more than any fundamental developments at the company.

Value Investing Is Predicated on the Efficient-Market Hypothesis Being Wrong

Investors should understand not only what value investing is but also why it is a successful investment philosophy. At the very core of its success is the recurrent mispricing of securities in the marketplace. Value investing is, in effect, predicated on the proposition that the efficient-market hypothesis is frequently wrong. If, on the one hand, securities can become undervalued or overvalued, which I believe to be incontrovertibly true, value investors will thrive. If, on the other hand, all securities at some future date become fairly and efficiently priced, value investors will have nothing to do. It is important, then, to consider whether or not the financial markets are efficient.

The efficient-market hypothesis takes three forms.[3] The weak form maintains that past stock prices provide no useful information on the future direction of stock prices. In other words, technical analysis (analysis of past price fluctuations) cannot help investors. The semistrong form says that *no* published information will help investors to select undervalued securities since the market has already discounted all publicly available information into securities prices. The strong form maintains that there is no information, public or private, that would benefit investors. The implication of both the semi-strong and strong forms is that fundamental analysis is useless. Investors might just as well select stocks at random.

Of the three forms of the efficient-market hypothesis, I believe that only the weak form is valid. Technical analysis is indeed a waste of time.

As to the other forms: yes, the market does tend to incorporate new information into prices—securities prices are neither random nor do they totally ignore available information—yet the market is far from efficient. There is simply no question that investors applying disciplined analysis can identify inefficiently priced securities, buy and sell accordingly, and achieve superior returns. Specifically, by finding securities whose prices depart appreciably from underlying value, investors can frequently achieve above-average returns while taking below-average risks.

The pricing of large-capitalization stocks tends to be more efficient than that of small-capitalization stocks, distressed bonds, and other less-popular investment fare. While hundreds of investment analysts follow IBM, few, if any, cover thousands of small-capitalization stocks and obscure junk bonds. Investors are more likely, therefore, to find inefficiently priced securities outside the Standard and Poor's 100 than within it. Even among the most highly capitalized issues, however, investors are frequently blinded by groupthink, thereby creating pricing inefficiencies.

Is it reasonable to expect that in the future some securities will continue to be significantly mispriced from time to time? I believe it is. The elegance of the efficient-market theory is at odds with the reality of how the financial markets operate.

An entire book could be written on this subject alone, but one enlightening article cleverly rebuts the efficient-market theory with living, breathing refutations. Buffett's "The Superinvestors of Graham-and-Doddsville" demonstrates how nine value-investment disciples of Benjamin Graham, holding varied and independent portfolios, achieved phenomenal investment success over long periods.[4]

Buffett considers the possibility that the extraordinary performance of these investors could somehow be a random event, such as correctly calling a sequence of coin tosses, or that the value investors discussed in his article comprise a biased sample, imitating rather than emulating Graham's investment strategy. Buffett strongly argues otherwise. His view is that the only thing the many value investors have in common is a philosophy that dictates the purchase of securities at a discount from underlying value. The existence of so many independent successes is inconsistent with the efficient-market theory. If the markets were efficient, then how could so many investors, identifiable by Buffett years ago as sharing a common philosophy but having little overlap in their portfolios, all have done so well? Buffett's argument has never, to my knowledge, been addressed by the efficient-market theorists; they evidently prefer to continue to prove in theory what is refuted in reality.

Why do stock prices tend to depart from underlying value, thereby making the financial markets inefficient? There are numerous reasons, the most obvious being that securities prices are determined in the short run by supply and demand. The forces of supply and demand do not necessarily correlate with value at any given time. Also, many buyers and sellers of securities are motivated by considerations other than underlying value and may be willing to buy or sell at very different prices than a value investor would.

If a stock is part of a major market index, for example, there will be demand from index funds to buy it regardless of whether it is overpriced in relation to underlying value. Similarly, if a stock has recently risen on increasing volume, technical analysts might consider it attractive; by definition, underlying value would not be a part of their calculations. If a company has exhibited rapid recent growth, it may trade at a "growth" multiple, far higher than a value investor would pay. Conversely, a company that recently reported disappointing results might be dumped by investors who focused exclusively on earnings, depressing the price to a level considerably below underlying value. An investor unable to meet a margin call is in no position to hold out for full value; he or she is forced to sell at the prevailing market price.

The behavior of institutional investors, dictated by constraints on their behavior, can sometimes cause stock prices to depart from underlying value. Institutional selling of a low-priced small-capitalization spinoff, for example, can cause a temporary supply-demand imbalance, resulting in a security becoming undervalued. If a company fails to declare an expected dividend, institutions restricted to owning only dividend-paying stocks may unload the shares. Bond funds allowed to own only investment-grade debt would dump their holdings of an issue immediately after it was downgraded below BBB by the rating agencies. Such phenomena as year-end tax selling and quarterly window dressing can also cause market inefficiencies, as value considerations are subordinated to other factors.

Benjamin Graham and David Dodd explained stock mispricings this way: "The market is not a weighing machine, on which the value of each issue is recorded by an exact and impersonal mechanism, in accordance with its specific qualities...The market is a voting machine, whereon countless individuals register choices which are the product partly of reason and partly of emotion."[5]

A central tenet of value investing is that over time the general tendency is for underlying value either to be reflected in securities prices or otherwise realized by shareholders. This does not mean that in the future stock prices will exactly equal underlying value. Some securities are always moving away from underlying value, while others are moving closer, and any given security is likely to be both undervalued and overvalued as well as fairly valued within its lifetime. The long-term expectation, however, is for the prices of securities to move toward underlying value.

Of course, securities are rarely priced in complete disregard of underlying value. Many of the forces that cause securities prices to depart from underlying value are temporary. In addition, there are a number of forces that help bring security prices into line with underlying value. Management prerogatives such as share issuance or repurchase, subsidiary spinoffs, recapitalizations, and, as a last resort, liquidation or sale of the business all can serve to narrow the gap between price and value. External forces such as hostile takeovers and proxy fights may also serve as catalysts to correct price/value disparities.

In a sense, value investing is a large-scale arbitrage between security prices and underlying business value. Arbitrage is a means of exploiting price differentials between markets. If gold sells for $400 per ounce in the U.S. and 260 pounds per ounce in the U.K. and the current exchange rate is $1.50 to the pound, an arbitrageur would convert $390 into pounds, purchase an ounce of gold in the U.K. and simultaneously sell it in the U.S., making a $10 profit less any transaction costs. Unlike classic arbitrage, however, value investing is not risk-free; profits are neither instantaneous nor certain.

Value arbitrage can occasionally be fairly simple. When a closed-end mutual fund trades at a significant discount to underlying value, for example, a majority of shareholders can force it to become open-ended (whereby shares can be redeemed at net asset value) or to liquidate, delivering underlying value directly to shareholders. The open-ending or liquidation of a closed-end fund is one of the purest examples of value arbitrage.

The arbitrage profit from purchasing the undervalued stock of an ongoing business can be more difficult to realize. The degree of difficulty in a given instance depends, among other things, on the magnitude of the gap between price and value, the extent to which management is entrenched, the identity and ownership position of the major shareholders, and the availability of credit in the economy for corporate takeover activity.

Beware of Value Pretenders

"Value investing" is one of the most overused and inconsistently applied terms in the investment business. A broad range of strategies make use of value investing as a pseudonym. Many have little or nothing to do with the philosophy of investing originally espoused by Graham. The misuse of the value label accelerated in the mid-1980s in the wake of increasing publicity given to the long-term successes of true value investors such as Buffett at Berkshire Hathaway, Inc., Michael Price and the late Max L. Heine at Mutual Series Fund, Inc., and William Ruane and Richard Cunniff at the Sequoia Fund, Inc., among others. Their results attracted a great many "value pretenders," investment chameleons who frequently change strategies in order to attract funds to manage.

These value pretenders are not true value investors, disciplined craftspeople who understand and accept the wisdom of the value approach. Rather they are charlatans who violate the conservative dictates of value investing, using inflated business valuations, overpaying for securities, and failing to achieve a margin of safety for their clients. These investors, despite (or perhaps as a direct result of) their imprudence, are able to achieve good investment results in times of rising markets. During the latter half of the 1980s, value pretenders gained widespread acceptance, earning high, even spectacular, returns. Many of them benefitted from the overstated private-market values that were prevalent during those years; when business valuations returned to historical levels in 1990, however, most value pretenders suffered substantial losses.

To some extent value, like beauty, is in the eye of the beholder; virtually any security may appear to be a bargain to someone. It is hard to prove an overly optimistic investor wrong in the short run since value is not precisely measurable and since stocks can remain overvalued for a long time. Accordingly, the buyer of virtually any security can claim to be a value investor at least for a while.

Ironically, many true value investors fell into disfavor during the late 1980s. As they avoided participating in the fully valued and overvalued securities that the value pretenders claimed to be bargains, many of them temporarily underperformed the results achieved by the value pretenders. The most conservative were actually criticized for their "excessive" caution, prudence that proved well founded in 1990.

Even today many of the value pretenders have not been defrocked of their value-investor mantle. There were many articles in financial periodicals chronicling the poor investment results posted by many so-called value investors in 1990. The top of the list, needless to say, was dominated by value pretenders.

Conclusion

Value investing is simple to understand but difficult to implement. Value investors are not supersophisticated analytical wizards who create and apply intricate computer models to find attractive opportunities or assess underlying value. The hard part is discipline, patience, and judgment. Investors need discipline to avoid the many unattractive pitches that are thrown, patience to wait for the right pitch, and judgment to know when it is time to swing.

Notes

1. Benjamin Graham, *The Intelligent Investor*, 4th ed. (New York: Harper & Row, 1973), p. 281.
2. Warren E. Buffett, "The Superinvestors of Graham-and-Doddsville," *Hermes* (Columbia Business School magazine) (Fall 1984):4–15.
3. Burton G. Malkiel, *A Random Walk down Wall Street*, 4th ed. (New York: W. W. Norton, 1985), pp. 174–75.
4. Buffett, pp.14–15.
5. Benjamin Graham, David L. Dodd, and Sidney Cottle, *Security Analysis* (New York: McGraw-Hill, 1962), p. 42.

7

At the Root of a Value-Investment Philosophy

There are three central elements to a value-investment philosophy. First, value investing is a bottom-up strategy entailing the identification of specific undervalued investment opportunities. Second, value investing is absolute-performance-, not relative-performance oriented. Finally, value investing is a risk-averse approach; attention is paid as much to what can go wrong (risk) as to what can go right (return).

The Merits of Bottom-Up Investing

In the discussion of institutional investing in chapter 3, it was noted that a great many professional investors employ a top-down approach. This involves making a prediction about the future, ascertaining its investment implications, and then acting upon them. This approach is difficult and risky, being vulnerable to error at every step. Practitioners need to accurately forecast macroeconomic conditions and then correctly interpret their impact on various sectors of the overall economy, on particular industries, and finally on specific companies. As if that were not complicated enough, it is also essential for top-down investors to perform this exercise quickly as well as accurately, or others may get there first and, through their buying or selling, cause prices to reflect the forecast macroeconomic developments, thereby eliminating the profit potential for latecomers.

By way of example, a top-down investor must be correct on the big picture (e.g., are we entering an unprecedented era of world peace and stability?), correct in drawing conclusions from that (e.g., is German reunification bullish or bearish for German interest rates and the value of the deutsche mark), correct in applying those conclusions to attractive areas of investment (e.g., buy German bonds, buy the stocks of U.S. companies with multinational presence), correct in the specific securities purchased (e.g., buy the ten-year German government bond, buy Coca-Cola), and, finally, be early in buying these securities.

The top-down investor thus faces the daunting task of predicting the unpredictable more accurately and faster than thousands of other bright people, all of them trying to do the same thing. It is not clear whether top-down investing is a greater-fool game, in which you win only when someone else overpays, or a greater-genius game, winnable at best only by those few who regularly possess superior insight. In either case, it is not an attractive game for risk-averse investors.

There is no margin of safety in top-down investing. Top-down investors are not buying based on value; they are buying based on a concept, theme, or trend. There is no definable limit to the price they should pay, since value is not part of their purchase decision. It is not even clear whether top-down-oriented buyers are investors or speculators. If they buy shares in businesses that they truly believe will do well in the future, they are investing. If they buy what they believe others will soon be buying, they may actually be speculating.

Another difficulty with a top-down approach is gauging the level of expectations already reflected in a company's current share price. If you expect a business to grow 10 percent a year based on your top-down forecast and buy its stock betting on that growth, you could lose money if the market price reflects investor expectations of 15 percent growth but a lower rate is achieved. The expectations of others must therefore be considered as part of any top-down investment decision. (See the discussion of torpedo stocks in chapter 6.)

By contrast, value investing employs a bottom-up strategy by which individual investment opportunities are identified one at a time through fundamental analysis. Value investors search for bargains security by security, analyzing each situation on its own merits. An investor's top-down views are considered only insofar as they affect the valuation of securities.

Paradoxically a bottom-up strategy is in many ways simpler to implement than a top-down one. While a top-down investor must make several accurate predictions in a row, a bottom-up investor is not in the forecasting business at all. The entire strategy can be concisely described as "buy a bargain and wait." Investors must learn to assess value in order to know a bargain when they see one. Then they must exhibit the patience and discipline to wait until a bargain emerges from their searches and buy it, regardless of the prevailing direction of the market or their own views about the economy at large.

One significant and not necessarily obvious difference between a bottom-up and top-down strategy is the reason for maintaining cash balances at times. Bottom-up investors hold cash when they are unable to find attractive investment opportunities and put cash to work when such opportunities appear. A bottom-up investor chooses to be fully invested only when a diversified portfolio of attractive investments is available. Top-down investors, by contrast, may attempt to time the market, something bottom-up investors do not do. Market timing involves making a judgment about the overall market direction; when top-down investors believe the market will decline, they sell stocks to hold cash, awaiting a more bullish opinion.

Another difference between the two approaches is that bottom-up investors are able to identify simply and precisely what they are betting on. The uncertainties they face are limited: what is the underlying business worth; will that underlying value endure until shareholders can benefit from its realization; what is the likelihood that the gap between price and value will narrow; and, given the current market price, what is the potential risk and reward?

Bottom-up investors can easily determine when the original reason for making an investment ceases to be valid. When the underlying value changes, when management reveals itself to be incompetent or corrupt, or when the price appreciates to more fully reflect underlying business value, a disciplined investor can reevaluate the situation and, if appropriate, sell the investment. Huge sums have been lost by investors who have held on to securities after the reason for owning them is no longer valid. In investing it is never wrong to change your mind. It is only wrong to change your mind and do nothing about it.

Top-down investors, by contrast, may find it difficult to know when their bet is no longer valid. If you invest based on a judgment that interest rates will decline but they rise instead, how and when do you decide that you were wrong? Your bet may eventually prove correct, but then again it may not. Unlike judgments about value that can easily be reaffirmed, the possible grounds for reversing an investment decision that was made based upon a top-down prediction of the future are simply not clear.

Adopt an Absolute-Performance Orientation

Most institutional and many individual investors have adopted a relative-performance orientation (as discussed in chapter 3). They invest with the goal of outperforming either the market, other investors, or both and are apparently indifferent as to whether the results achieved represent an absolute gain or loss. Good relative performance, especially short-term relative performance, is commonly sought either by imitating what others are doing or by attempting to outguess what others will do. Value investors, by contrast, are absolute-performance oriented; they are interested in returns only insofar as they relate to the achievement of their own investment goals, not how they compare with the way the overall market or other investors are faring. Good absolute performance is obtained by purchasing undervalued securities while selling holdings that become more fully valued. For most investors absolute returns are the only ones that really matter; you cannot, after all, spend relative performance.

Absolute-performance-oriented investors usually take a longer-term perspective than relative-performance-oriented investors. A relative-performance-oriented investor is generally unwilling or unable to tolerate long periods of underperformance and therefore invests in whatever is currently popular. To do otherwise would jeopardize near-term results. Relative-performance-oriented investors may actually shun situations that clearly offer attractive absolute returns over the long run if making them would risk near-term underperformance. By contrast, absolute-performance-oriented investors are likely to prefer out-of-favor holdings that may take longer to come to fruition but also carry less risk of loss.

One significant difference between an absolute- and relative-performance orientation is evident in the different strategies for investing available cash. Relative-performance-oriented investors will typically choose to be fully invested at all times, since cash balances would likely cause them to lag behind a rising market. Since the goal is at least to match and optimally beat the market, any cash that is not promptly spent on specific investments must nevertheless be invested in a market-related index.

Absolute-performance-oriented investors, by contrast, are willing to hold cash reserves when no bargains are available. Cash is liquid and provides a modest, sometimes attractive nominal return, usually above the rate of inflation. The liquidity of cash affords flexibility, for it can quickly be channeled into other investment outlets with minimal transaction costs. Finally, unlike any other holding, cash does not involve any risk of incurring opportunity cost (losses from the inability to take advantage of future bargains) since it does not drop in value during market declines.

Risk and Return

While most other investors are preoccupied with how much money they can make and not at all with how much they may lose, value investors focus on risk as well as return. To the extent that most investors think about risk at all, they seem confused about it. Some insist that risk and return are *always* positively correlated; the greater the risk, the greater the return. This is, in fact, a basic tenet of the capital-asset-pricing model taught in nearly all business schools, yet it is not always true. Others mistakenly equate risk with volatility, emphasizing the "risk" of security price fluctuations while ignoring the risk of making overpriced, ill-conceived, or poorly managed investments.

A positive correlation between risk and return would hold consistently only in an efficient market. Any disparities would be immediately corrected; this is what would make the market efficient. In inefficient markets it is possible to find investments offering high returns with low risk. These arise when information is not widely available, when an investment is particularly complicated to analyze, or when investors buy and sell for reasons unrelated to value. It is also commonplace to discover high-risk investments offering low returns. Overpriced and therefore risky investments are often available because the financial markets are biased toward overvaluation and because it is difficult for market forces to correct an overvalued condition if enough speculators persist in overpaying. Also, unscrupulous operators will always make overpriced investments available to anyone willing to buy; they are not legally required to sell at a fair price.

Since the financial markets are inefficient a good deal of the time, investors cannot simply select a level of risk and be confident that it will be reflected in the accompanying returns. Risk and return must instead be assessed independently for every investment.

In point of fact, greater risk does not guarantee greater return. To the contrary, risk erodes return by causing losses. It is only when investors shun high-risk investments, thereby depressing their prices, that an incremental return can be earned which more than fully compensates for the risk incurred. By itself risk does not create incremental return; only price can accomplish that.

The Nature of Risk

The risk of an investment is described by both the probability and the potential amount of loss. The risk of an investment—the probability of an adverse outcome—is partly inherent in its very nature. A dollar spent on biotechnology research is a riskier investment than a dollar used to purchase utility equipment. The former has both a greater probability of loss and a greater percentage of the investment at stake.

In the financial markets, however, the connection between a marketable security and the underlying business is not as clearcut. For investors in a marketable security the gain or loss associated with the various outcomes is not totally inherent in the underlying business; it also depends on the price paid, which is established by the marketplace. The view that risk is dependent on both the nature of investments and on their market price is very different from that described by beta (which is considered in the next section).

While security analysts attempt to determine with precision the risk and return of investments, events alone accomplish that. For most investments the amount of profit earned can be known only after maturity or sale. Only for the safest of investments is return knowable at the time of purchase: a one-year 6 percent T-bill returns 6 percent at the end of one year. For riskier investments the outcome must be known before the return can be calculated. If you buy one hundred shares of Chrysler Corporation, for example, your return depends almost entirely on the price at which it is trading when you sell. Only then can the return be calculated.

Unlike return, however, risk is no more quantifiable at the end of an investment than it was at its beginning. Risk simply cannot be described by a single number. Intuitively we understand that risk varies from investment to investment: a government bond is not as risky as the stock of a high-technology company. But investments do not provide information about their risks the way food packages provide nutritional data.

Rather, risk is a perception in each investor's mind that results from analysis of the probability and amount of potential loss from an investment. If an exploratory oil well proves to be a dry hole, it is called risky. If a bond defaults or a stock plunges in price, they are called risky. But if the well is a gusher, the bond matures on schedule, and the stock rallies strongly, can we say they weren't risky when the investment was made? Not at all. The point is, in most cases no more is known about the risk of an investment after it is concluded than was known when it was made.

There are only a few things investors can do to counteract risk: diversify adequately, hedge when appropriate, and invest with a margin of safety. It is precisely because we do not and cannot know all the risks of an investment that we strive to invest at a discount. The bargain element helps to provide a cushion for when things go wrong.

For Beta or Worse

Many market participants believe that investment risk is intrinsic to specific securities, as it is to activities like hang gliding and mountain climbing. Using modern financial theory, academics and many market professionals have attempted to quantify this risk with a single statistical measure, beta. Beta compares a security's or portfolio's historical price fluctuations with those of the market as a whole. High-beta stocks are defined as those that tend to rise by a higher percentage than the average stock in a rising market and decline more than the average stock in a falling market. Due to their greater volatility, high-beta stocks are deemed to be riskier than low-beta stocks.

I find it preposterous that a single number reflecting past price fluctuations could be thought to completely describe the risk in a security. Beta views risk solely from the perspective of market prices, failing to take into consideration specific business fundamentals or economic developments. The price level is also ignored, as if IBM selling at 50 dollars per share would not be a lower-risk investment than the same IBM at 100 dollars per share. Beta fails to allow for the influence that investors themselves can exert on the riskiness of their holdings through such efforts as proxy contests, shareholder resolutions, communications with management, or the ultimate purchase of sufficient stock to gain corporate control and with it direct access to underlying value. Beta also assumes that the upside potential and downside risk of any investment are essentially equal, being simply a function of that investment's volatility compared with that of the market as a whole. This too is inconsistent with the world as we know it. The reality is that past security price volatility does not reliably predict future investment performance (or even future volatility) and therefore is a poor measure of risk.

The Relevance of Temporary Price Fluctuations

In addition to the probability of permanent loss attached to an investment, there is also the possibility of interim price fluctuations that are unrelated to underlying value. (Beta fails to distinguish between the two.) Many investors consider price fluctuations to be a significant risk: if the price goes down, the investment is seen as risky regardless of the fundamentals. But are temporary price fluctuations really a risk? Not in the way that permanent value impairments are and then only for certain investors in specific situations.

It is, of course, not always easy for investors to distinguish temporary price volatility, related to the short-term forces of supply and demand, from price movements related to business fundamentals. The reality may only become apparent after the fact. While investors should obviously try to avoid overpaying for investments or buying into businesses that subsequently decline in value due to deteriorating results, it is not possible to avoid random short-term market volatility. Indeed, investors should expect prices to fluctuate and should not invest in securities if they cannot tolerate some volatility.

If you are buying sound value at a discount, do short-term price fluctuations matter? In the long run they do not matter much; value will ultimately be reflected in the price of a security. Indeed, ironically, the long-term investment implication of price fluctuations is in the opposite direction from the near-term market impact. For example, short-term price declines actually enhance the returns of long-term investors.[1] There are, however, several eventualities in which near-term price fluctuations do matter to investors. Security holders who need to sell in a hurry are at the mercy of market prices. The trick of successful investors is to sell when they want to, not when they have to. Investors who may need to sell should not own marketable securities other than U.S. Treasury bills.

Near-term security prices also matter to investors in a troubled company. If a business must raise additional capital in the near term to survive, investors in its securities may have their fate determined, at least in part, by the prevailing market price of the company's stock and bonds. (Chapter 8 contains a more complete discussion of this effect, known as reflexivity.)

The third reason long-term-oriented investors are interested in short-term price fluctuations is that Mr. Market can create very attractive opportunities to buy and sell. If you hold cash, you are able to take advantage of such opportunities. If you are fully invested when the market declines, your portfolio will likely drop in value, depriving you of the benefits arising from the opportunity to buy in at lower levels. This creates an opportunity cost, the necessity to forego future opportunities that arise. If what you hold is illiquid or unmarketable, the opportunity cost increases further; the illiquidity precludes your switching to better bargains.

The most important determinant of whether investors will incur opportunity cost is whether or not part of their portfolios is held in cash. Maintaining moderate cash balances or owning securities that periodically throw off appreciable cash is likely to reduce the number of foregone opportunities. Investors can manage portfolio cash flow (defined as the cash flowing into a portfolio minus outflows) by giving preference to some kinds of investments over others. Portfolio cash flow is greater for securities of shorter duration (weighted average life) than those of longer duration. Portfolio cash flow is also enhanced by investments with catalysts for the partial or complete realization of underlying value (discussed at greater length in chapter 10). Equity investments in ongoing businesses typically throw off only minimal cash through the payment of dividends. The securities of companies in bankruptcy and liquidation, by contrast, can return considerable liquidity to a portfolio within a few years of purchase. Risk-arbitrage investments typically have very short lives, usually turning back into cash, liquid securities, or both in a matter of weeks or months. An added attraction of investing in risk-arbitrage situations, bankruptcies, and liquidations is that not only is one's initial investment returned to cash, one's profits are as well.

Another way to limit opportunity cost is through hedging. A hedge is an investment that is expected to move in a direction opposite that of another holding so as to cushion any price decline. If the hedge becomes valuable, it can be sold, providing funds to take advantage of newly created opportunities. (Hedging is discussed in greater depth in chapter 13.)

Conclusion

The primary goal of value investors is to avoid losing money. Three elements of a value-investment strategy make achievement of that goal possible. A bottom-up approach, searching for low-risk bargains one at a time through fundamental analysis, is the surest way I know to avoid losing money. An absolute-performance orientation is consistent with loss avoidance; a relative-performance orientation is not. Finally, paying careful attention to risk—the probability and amount of loss due to permanent value impairments—will help investors avoid losing money. So long as generating portfolio cash inflow is not inconsistent with earning acceptable returns, investors can reduce the opportunity cost resulting from interim price declines even as they achieve their long-term investment goals.

Notes

1. Consider the example of a five-year 10 percent bond paying interest semiannually which is purchased at par ($100). Assuming that interest rates remain unchanged over the life of the bond, interest coupons can also be invested at 10 percent, resulting in an annual rate of return of 10 percent for that bond. If immediately after the bond is purchased, interest rates decline to 5 percent, the bond will initially rise to $121.88 from $100. The bond rises in price to reflect the present value of 10 percent interest coupons discounted at a 5 percent interest rate over five years. The bond could be sold for a profit of nearly 22 percent. However, if the investor decides to hold the bond to maturity, the annualized return will be only 9.10 percent. This is less than in the flat interest case because the interest coupons are reinvested at 5 percent, not 10 percent. Despite the potential short-term profit from a decline in interest rates, the return to the investor who holds on to the bonds is actually reduced.

   Similarly, if interest rates rise to 15 percent immediately after purchase, the investor is faced with a market decline from par to $82.84, a 17 percent loss. The total return, if he holds the bond for 5 years, is increased, however, to 10.99 percent as coupons are reinvested at 15 percent. This example demon-strates how the short-term and long-term perspectives on an investment can diverge. In a rising market, many people feel wealthy due to unrealized capital gains, but they are likely to be worse off over the long run than if security prices had remained lower and the returns to incremental investment higher.

8

The Art of Business Valuation

Many investors insist on affixing exact values to their investments, seeking precision in an imprecise world, but business
value cannot be precisely determined. Reported book value,
earnings, and cash flow are, after all, only the best guesses of
accountants who follow a fairly strict set of standards and practices designed more to achieve conformity than to reflect economic value. Projected results are less precise still. You cannot
appraise the value of your home to the nearest thousand dollars. Why would it be any easier to place a value on vast and
complex businesses?

Not only is business value imprecisely knowable, it also
changes over time, fluctuating with numerous macroeconomic,
microeconomic, and market-related factors. So while investors
at any given time cannot determine business value with precision, they must nevertheless almost continuously reassess their
estimates of value in order to incorporate all known factors that
could influence their appraisal.

Any attempt to value businesses with precision will yield
values that are precisely inaccurate. The problem is that it is

easy to confuse the capability to make precise forecasts with the ability to make accurate ones. Anyone with a simple, hand-held calculator can perform net present value (NPV) and internal rate of return (IRR) calculations. The NPV calculation provides a single-point value of an investment by discounting estimates of future cash flow back to the present. IRR, using assumptions of future cash flow and price paid, is a calculation of the rate of return on an investment to as many decimal places as desired. The seeming precision provided by NPV and IRR calculations can give investors a false sense of certainty for they are really only as accurate as the cash flow assumptions that were used to derive them.

The advent of the computerized spreadsheet has exacerbated this problem, creating the illusion of extensive and thoughtful analysis, even for the most haphazard of efforts. Typically, investors place a great deal of importance on the output, even though they pay little attention to the assumptions. "Garbage in, garbage out" is an apt description of the process.

NPV and IRR are wonderful at summarizing, in absolute and percentage terms, respectively, the returns for a given series of cash flows. When cash flows are contractually determined, as in the case of a bond, and when all payments are received when due, IRR provides the precise rate of return to the investor while NPV describes the value of the investment at a given discount rate. In the case of a bond, these calculations allow investors to quantify their returns under one set of assumptions, that is, that contractual payments are received when due. These tools, however, are of no use in determining the likelihood that investors will actually receive all contractual payments and, in fact, achieve the projected returns.

A Range of Value

Businesses, unlike debt instruments, do not have contractual cash flows. As a result, they cannot be as precisely valued as bonds. Benjamin Graham knew how hard it is to pinpoint the value of businesses and thus of equity securities that represent fractional ownership of those businesses. In *Security Analysis* he and David Dodd discussed the concept of a range of value:

> The essential point is that security analysis does not seek to determine exactly what is the intrinsic value of a given security. It needs only to establish that the value is adequate—e.g., to protect a bond or to justify a stock purchase—or else that the value is considerably higher or considerably lower than the market price. For such purposes an indefinite and approximate measure of the intrinsic value may be sufficient.[1]

Indeed, Graham frequently performed a calculation known as net working capital per share, a back-of-the-envelope estimate of a company's liquidation value. His use of this rough approximation was a tacit admission that he was often unable to ascertain a company's value more precisely.

To illustrate the difficulty of accurate business valuation, investors need only consider the wide range of Wall Street estimates that typically are offered whenever a company is put up for sale. In 1989, for example, Campeau Corporation marketed Bloomingdales to prospective buyers; Harcourt Brace Jovanovich, Inc., held an auction of its Sea World subsidiary; and Hilton Hotels, Inc., offered itself for sale. In each case Wall Street's value estimates ranged widely, with the highest estimate as much as twice the lowest figure. If expert analysts with extensive information cannot gauge the value of high-profile, well-regarded businesses with more certainty than this, investors should not fool themselves into believing they are capable of greater precision when buying marketable securities based only on limited, publicly available information.

Markets exist because of differences of opinion among investors. If securities could be valued precisely, there would be many fewer differences of opinion; market prices would fluctuate less frequently, and trading activity would diminish. To fundamentally oriented investors, the value of a security to the buyer must be greater than the price paid, and the value to the seller must be less, or no transaction would take place. The discrepancy between the buyer's and the seller's perceptions of value can result from such factors as differences in assumptions regarding the future, different intended uses for the asset, and differences in the discount rates applied. Every asset being bought and sold thus has a possible range of values bounded by the value to the buyer and the value to the seller; the actual transaction price will be somewhere in between.

In early 1991, for example, the junk bonds of Tonka Corporation sold at steep discounts to par value, and the stock sold for a few dollars per share. The company was offered for sale by its investment bankers, and Hasbro, Inc., was evidently willing to pay more for Tonka than any other buyer because of economies that could be achieved in combining the two operations. Tonka, in effect, provided appreciably higher cash flows to Hasbro than it would have generated either as a stand-alone business or to most other buyers. There was a sharp difference of opinion between the financial markets and Hasbro regarding the value of Tonka, a disagreement that was resolved with Hasbro's acquisition of the company.

Business Valuation

To be a value investor, you must buy at a discount from underlying value. Analyzing each potential value investment opportunity therefore begins with an assessment of business value.

While a great many methods of business valuation exist, there are only three that I find useful. The first is an analysis of going-concern value, known as net present value (NPV) analysis. NPV is the discounted value of all future cash flows that a business is expected to generate. A frequently used but flawed shortcut method of valuing a going concern is known as private-market value. This is an investor's assessment of the price that a sophisticated businessperson would be willing to pay for a business. Investors using this shortcut, in effect, value businesses using the multiples paid when comparable busi-nesses were previously bought and sold in their entirety.

The second method of business valuation analyzes liquida-tion value, the expected proceeds if a company were to be dis-mantled and the assets sold off. Breakup value, one variant of liquidation analysis, considers each of the components of a business at its highest valuation, whether as part of a going con-cern or not.

The third method of valuation, stock market value, is an esti-mate of the price at which a company, or its subsidiaries consid-ered separately, would trade in the stock market. Less reliable than the other two, this method is only occasionally useful as a yardstick of value.

Each of these methods of valuation has strengths and weak-nesses. None of them provides accurate values all the time. Unfortunately no better methods of valuation exist. Investors have no choice but to consider the values generated by each of them; when they appreciably diverge, investors should gener-ally err on the side of conservatism.

Present-Value Analysis and the Difficulty of Forecasting Future Cash Flow

When future cash flows[2] are reasonably predictable and an appropriate discount rate can be chosen, NPV analysis is one of the most accurate and precise methods of valuation. Unfortunately future cash flows are usually uncertain, often highly so. Moreover, the choice of a discount rate can be some-what arbitrary. These factors together typically make present-value analysis an imprecise and difficult task.

A perfect business in terms of the simplicity of valuation would be an annuity; an annuity generates an annual stream of cash that either remains constant or grows at a steady rate every year. Real businesses, even the best ones, are unfortunately not annuities. Few businesses occupy impenetrable market niches and generate consistently high returns, and most are subject to intense competition. Small changes in either revenues or expenses cause far greater percentage changes in profits. The number of things that can go wrong greatly exceeds the number that can go right. Responding to business uncertainty is the job of corporate management. However, controlling or preventing uncertainty is generally beyond management's ability and should not be expected by investors.[3]

Although some businesses are more stable than others and therefore more predictable, estimating future cash flow for a business is usually a guessing game. A recurring theme in this book is that the future is not predictable, except within fairly wide boundaries. Will Coca-Cola sell soda next year? Of course. Will it sell more than this year? Pretty definitely, since it has done so every year since 1980. How much more is not so clear. How much the company will earn from selling it is even less clear; factors such as pricing, the sensitivity of demand to changes in price, competitors' actions, and changes in corporate tax rates all may affect profitability. Forecasting sales or profits many years into the future is considerably more imprecise, and a great many factors can derail any business forecast.

There are many investors who make decisions solely on the basis of their own forecasts of future growth. After all, the faster the earnings or cash flow of a business is growing, the greater that business's present value. Yet several difficulties confront growth-oriented investors. First, such investors frequently demonstrate higher confidence in their ability to predict the future than is warranted. Second, for fast-growing businesses even small differences in one's estimate of annual growth rates can have a tremendous impact on valuation.[4] Moreover, with so many investors attempting to buy stock in growth companies, the prices of the consensus choices may reach levels unsupported by fundamentals. Since entry to the "Business Hall of Fame" is frequently through a revolving door, investors may at times be lured into making overly optimistic projections based on temporarily robust results, thereby causing them to overpay for mediocre businesses. When growth is anticipated and therefore already discounted in securities prices, shortfalls will disappoint investors and result in share price declines. As Warren Buffett has said, "For the investor, a too-high purchase price for the stock of an excellent company can undo the effects of a subsequent decade of favorable business developments."[5]

Another difficulty with investing based on growth is that while investors tend to oversimplify growth into a single number, growth is, in fact, comprised of numerous moving parts which vary in their predictability. For any particular business, for example, earnings growth can stem from increased unit sales related to predictable increases in the general population, to increased usage of a product by consumers, to increased market share, to greater penetration of a product into the population, or to price increases. Specifically, a brewer might expect to sell more beer as the drinking-age population grows but would aspire to selling more beer per capita as well. Budweiser would hope to increase market share relative to Miller. The brewing industry might wish to convert whiskey drinkers into beer drinkers or reach the abstemious segment of the population with a brand of nonalcoholic beer. Over time companies would seek to increase price to the extent that it would be expected to result in increased profits.

Some of these sources of earnings growth are more predictable than others. Growth tied to population increases is considerably more certain than growth stemming from changes in consumer behavior, such as the conversion of whiskey drinkers to beer. The reaction of customers to price increases is always uncertain. On the whole it is far easier to identify the possible sources of growth for a business than to forecast how much growth will actually materialize and how it will affect profits.

An unresolvable contradiction exists: to perform present-value analysis, you must predict the future, yet the future is not reliably predictable. The miserable failure in 1990 of highly leveraged companies such as Southland Corporation and Interco, Inc., to meet their own allegedly reasonable projections made just a few years earlier—in both cases underperforming by more than 50 percent—highlights the difficulty of predicting the future even a few years ahead.

Investors are often overly optimistic in their assessment of the future. A good example of this is the common response to corporate write-offs. This accounting practice enables a company at its sole discretion to clean house, instantaneously ridding itself of underperforming assets, uncollectible receivables, bad loans, and the costs incurred in any corporate restructuring accompanying the write-off. Typically such moves are enthusiastically greeted by Wall Street analysts and investors alike; post-write-off the company generally reports a higher return on equity and better profit margins. Such improved results are then projected into the future, justifying a higher stock market valuation. Investors, however, should not so generously allow the slate to be wiped clean. When historical mistakes are erased, it is too easy to view the past as error free. It is then only a small additional step to project this error-free past forward into the future, making the improbable forecast that no currently profitable operation will go sour and that no poor investments will ever again be made.

How do value investors deal with the analytical necessity to predict the unpredictable? The only answer is conservatism. Since all projections are subject to error, optimistic ones tend to place investors on a precarious limb. Virtually everything must go right, or losses may be sustained. Conservative forecasts can be more easily met or even exceeded. Investors are well advised to make only conservative projections and then invest only at a substantial discount from the valuations derived therefrom.

The Choice of a Discount Rate

The other component of present-value analysis, choosing a discount rate, is rarely given sufficient consideration by investors. A discount rate is, in effect, the rate of interest that would make an investor indifferent between present and future dollars. [Investors with a strong preference for present over future consumption or with a preference for the certainty of the present to the uncertainty of the future would use a high rate for discounting their investments. Other investors may be more willing to take a chance on forecasts holding true; they would apply a low discount rate, one that makes future cash flows nearly as valuable as today's.]

There is no single correct discount rate for a set of future cash flows and no precise way to choose one. The appropriate discount rate for a particular investment depends not only on an investor's preference for present over future consumption but also on his or her own risk profile, on the perceived risk of the investment under consideration, and on the returns available from alternative investments.

Investors tend to oversimplify; the way they choose a discount rate is a good example of this. A great many investors routinely use 10 percent as an all-purpose discount rate regardless of the nature of the investment under consideration. Ten percent is a nice round number, easy to remember and apply, but it is not always a good choice.

The underlying risk of an investment's future cash flows must be considered in choosing the appropriate discount rate for that investment. A short-term, risk-free investment (if one exists) should be discounted at the yield available on short-term U.S. Treasury securities, which, as stated earlier, are considered a proxy for the risk-free interest rate.[6] Low-grade bonds, by contrast, are discounted by the market at rates of 12 to 15 percent or more, reflecting investors' uncertainty that the contractual cash flows will be paid.

It is essential that investors choose discount rates as conservatively as they forecast future cash flows. Depending on the timing and magnitude of the cash flows, even modest differences in the discount rate can have a considerable impact on the present-value calculation.

Business value is influenced by changes in discount rates and therefore by fluctuations in interest rates. While it would be easier to determine the value of investments if interest rates and thus discount rates were constant, investors must accept the fact that they do fluctuate and take what action they can to minimize the effect of interest rate fluctuations on their portfolios.

How can investors know the "correct" level of interest rates in choosing a discount rate? I believe there is no "correct" level of rates. They are what the market says they are, and no one can predict where they are headed. Mostly I give current, risk-free interest rates the benefit of the doubt and assume that they are correct. Like many other financial-market phenomena there is some cyclicality to interest rate fluctuations. High interest rates lead to changes in the economy that are precursors to lower interest rates and vice versa. Knowing this does not help one make particularly accurate forecasts, however, for it is almost impossible to envision the economic cycle until after the fact.

At times when interest rates are unusually low, however, investors are likely to find very high multiples being applied to share prices. Investors who pay these high multiples are dependent on interest rates remaining low, but no one can be certain that they will. This means that when interest rates are unusually low, investors should be particularly reluctant to commit capital to long-term holdings unless outstanding opportunities become available, with a preference for either holding cash or investing in short-term holdings that quickly return cash for possible redeployment when available returns are more attractive.

Investors can apply present-value analysis in one of two ways. They can calculate the present-value of a business and use it to place a value on its securities. Alternatively, they can calculate the present-value of the cash flows that security holders will receive: interest and principal payments in the case of bondholders and dividends and estimated future share prices in the case of stockholders.

Calculating the present value of contractual interest and principal payments is the best way to value a bond. Analysis of the underlying business can then help to establish the probability that those cash flows will be received. By contrast, analyzing the cash flows of the underlying business is the best way to value a stock. The only cash flows that investors typically receive from a stock are dividends. The dividend-discount method of valuation, which calculates the present value of a projected stream of future dividend payments, is not a useful tool for valuing equities; for most stocks, dividends constitute only a small fraction of total corporate cash flow and must be projected at least several decades into the future to give a meaningful approximation of business value. Accurately predicting that far ahead is an impossibility.

Once future cash flows are forecast conservatively and an appropriate discount rate is chosen, present value can be calculated. In theory, investors might assign different probabilities to numerous cash flow scenarios, then calculate the expected value of an investment, multiplying the probability of each scenario by its respective present value and then summing these numbers. In practice, given the extreme difficulty of assigning probabilities to numerous forecasts, investors make do with only a few likely scenarios. They must then perform sensitivity analysis in which they evaluate the effect of different cash flow forecasts and different discount rates on present value. If modest changes in assumptions cause a substantial change in net present value, investors would be prudent to exercise caution in employing this method of valuation.

Private-Market Value

A valuation method related to net present value is private-market value, which values businesses based on the valuation multiples that sophisticated, prudent businesspeople have recently paid to purchase similar businesses. Private-market value can provide investors with useful rules of thumb based on the economics of past transactions to guide them in business valuation. This valuation method is not without its shortcomings, however. Within a given business or industry all companies are not the same, but private-market value fails to distinguish among them. Moreover, the multiples paid to acquire businesses vary over time; valuations may have changed since the most recent similar transaction. Finally, buyers of businesses do not necessarily pay reasonable, intelligent prices.

The validity of private-market value depends on the assumption that businesspeople know what they are doing. In other words, when businesspeople consistently pay a certain multiple of revenues, earnings, or cash flow for a business, it is assumed that they are doing so after having performed an insightful analysis of the underlying economics. Often they have. After all, if the prices paid were routinely too high, the eventual losses incurred would inform subsequent buyers who would pay less in the future. If the prices paid were too low, the buyers would earn high returns; seeing this, others would eventually bid prices up to levels where excess profits could no longer be achieved. Nevertheless, the fact is that the prices paid by buyers of businesses can diverge from the underlying economics of those businesses for long stretches of time.

In the latter half of the 1980s, for example, the "private-market values" that investors came to rely on ceased to be the prices that sophisticated, prudent businesspeople would pay for businesses. Financiers armed with the proceeds of nonrecourse junk-bond offerings and using almost none of their own money were motivated by a tremendous skewing of their own risk and reward, as well as by enormous up-front fees, to overpay for corporate takeovers. Indeed, investors' assessment of private-market value in many cases became the price that a junk-bond-financed buyer might pay; investors failed to consider that those acquirers were starting to go bankrupt because the prices they had paid were excessive.

As the prices paid for businesses rose above historic multiples of underlying business value, traditional private-market buyers were shut out of the market. Television stations, which had been valued for many years at roughly ten times pretax cash flow, came to sell at prices as high as thirteen to fifteen times pretax cash flow. The prices of many other businesses with perceived consumer franchises became similarly inflated.

Investors who mistakenly equated inflated takeover prices with reliable private-market values were lured into overpaying for stocks and junk bonds in the mid-1980s. When nonrecourse financing became less freely available in 1989 and 1990, valuation multiples fell back to historic norms or below, causing these investors to experience substantial losses.

Nonrecourse debt is not the only skewing influence on private-market-value multiples. In the conglomerate boom of the late 1960s and early 1970s, for example, companies with extraordinarily high share prices used their overvalued equity as currency to buy other businesses. Undisciplined investors were lured into raising their own estimates of private-market values (even if they didn't use this terminology at the time), while ignoring the fact that these high valuations were dependent on ephemeral stock prices. When overvalued conglomerate shares slumped, takeover multiples followed suit.

Investors must ignore private-market values based upon inflated securities prices. Indeed, valuing securities based on the prices paid in takeovers that use securities as currency is circular reasoning, since higher security prices become a self-fulfilling prophecy. Investors relying on conservative historical standards of valuation in determining private-market value will benefit from a true margin of safety, while others' margin of safety blows with the financial winds.

How do sophisticated private-market buyers themselves evaluate businesses for possible purchase? In general, they make projections of free cash flow and then calculate the present value of those cash flows, evaluating the impact of differing assumptions on valuation. In other words, they perform present-value analysis.

What distinguishes private-market-value analysis from present-value analysis is the involvement of the middleman, the sophisticated businessperson, whose role has both positive and negative aspects. On the positive side, if the middleman makes a sizable financial commitment, this may help to corroborate the investors' own present-value analysis. On the negative side, relying on the judgment of a buyer of businesses, who may or may not be truly knowledgeable and insightful, can cause investors to become complacent and to neglect to perform their own independent valuations as a check. My personal rule is that investors should value businesses based on what they themselves, not others, would pay to own them. At most, private-market value should be used as one of several inputs in the valuation process and not as the exclusive final arbiter of value.

Liquidation Value

The liquidation value of a business is a conservative assessment of its worth in which only tangible assets are considered and intangibles, such as going-concern value, are not. Accordingly, when a stock is selling at a discount to liquidation value per share, a near rock-bottom appraisal, it is frequently an attractive investment.

A liquidation analysis is a theoretical exercise in valuation but not usually an actual approach to value realization. The assets of a company are typically worth more as part of a going concern than in liquidation, so liquidation value is generally a worst-case assessment. Even when an ongoing business is dismantled, many of its component parts are not actually liquidated but instead are sold intact as operating entities. Breakup value is one form of liquidation analysis; this involves determining the highest value of each component of a business, either as an ongoing enterprise or in liquidation. Most announced corporate liquidations are really breakups; ongoing business value is preserved whenever it exceeds liquidation value.

How should investors value assets in a liquidation analysis? An orderly liquidation over time is virtually certain to realize greater proceeds than a "fire sale," but time is not always available to a company in liquidation. When a business is in financial distress, a quick liquidation (a fire sale) may maximize the estate value. In a fire sale the value of inventory, depending on its nature, must be discounted steeply below carrying value. Receivables should probably be significantly discounted as well; the nature of the business, the identity of the customer, the amount owed, and whether or not the business is in any way ongoing all influence the ultimate realization from each receivable.

When no crisis is at hand, liquidation proceeds are usually maximized through a more orderly winding up of a business. In an orderly liquidation the values realized from disposing of current assets will more closely approximate stated book value. Cash, as in any liquidation analysis, is worth one hundred cents on the dollar. Investment securities should be valued at market prices, less estimated transaction costs in selling them. Accounts receivable are appraised at close to their face amount. The realizable value of inventories—tens of thousands of programmed computer diskettes, hundreds of thousands of purple sneakers, or millions of sticks of chewing gum—is not so easily determinable and may well be less than book value. The discount depends on whether the inventories consist of finished goods, work in process, or raw materials, and whether or not there is the risk of technological or fashion obsolescence. The value of the inventory in a supermarket does not fluctuate much, but the value of a warehouse full of computers certainly may. Obviously, a liquidation sale would yield less for inventory than would an orderly sale to regular customers.

The liquidation value of a company's fixed assets can be difficult to determine. The value of plant and equipment, for example, depends on its ability to generate cash flows, either in the current use or in alternative uses. Some machines and facilities are multipurpose and widely owned; others may have value only to the present owner. The value of restaurant equipment, for example, is more readily determinable than the value of an aging steel mill.

In approximating the liquidation value of a company, some value investors, emulating Benjamin Graham, calculate "net-net working capital" as a shortcut. Net working capital consists of current assets (cash, marketable securities, receivables, and inventories) less current liabilities (accounts, notes, and taxes payable within one year.) Net-net working capital is defined as net working capital minus all long-term liabilities. Even when a company has little ongoing business value, investors who buy at a price below net-net working capital are protected by the approximate liquidation value of current assets alone. As long as working capital is not overstated and operations are not rapidly consuming cash, a company could liquidate its assets, extinguish all its liabilities, and still distribute proceeds in excess of the market price to investors. Ongoing business losses can, however, quickly erode net-net working capital. Investors must therefore always consider the state of a company's current operations before buying. Investors should also consider any off-balance sheet or contingent liabilities, such as underfunded pension plans, as well as any liabilities that might be incurred in the course of an actual liquidation, such as plant closing and environmental laws.

A corporate liquidation typically connotes business failure; but ironically, it may correspond with investment success. The reason is that the liquidation or breakup of a company is a catalyst for the realization of underlying business value. Since value investors attempt to buy securities trading at a considerable discount from the value of a business's underlying assets, a liquidation is one way for investors to realize profits.

A liquidation is, in a sense, one of the few interfaces where the essence of the stock market is revealed. Are stocks pieces of paper to be endlessly traded back and forth, or are they proportional interests in underlying businesses? A liquidation settles this debate, distributing to owners of pieces of paper the actual cash proceeds resulting from the sale of corporate assets to the highest bidder. A liquidation thereby acts as a tether to reality for the stock market, forcing either undervalued or overvalued share prices to move into line with actual underlying value.

Stock Market Value

Occasionally investors must rely on the public equity and debt markets to provide an approximation of the worth of a security. Sometimes, as in the case of a closed-end mutual fund, this is the only relevant valuation method. Other times, especially if the time frame in which the value must be realized is short, the stock market method may be the best of several poor alternatives.

Consider the valuation of an investment company. In mid-1990 the Schaefer Value Trust, Inc., a closed-end mutual fund, scheduled a vote of its shareholders to consider liquidation. The most relevant measure of the liquidation value of Schaefer was its stock market value, the value that its holdings would bring when sold at once in the stock market. No other valuation method would have been appropriate.

Stock market value applies in other situations as well. In attempting to value a company's interest in an unrelated subsidiary or joint venture, for example, investors would certainly consider the discounted anticipated future cash flow stream (net present value), the valuation of comparable businesses in transactions (private-market value), and the value of tangible assets net of liabilities (liquidation value). Investors would also benefit from considering stock market value, the valuation of comparable businesses in the stock market. While the stock market's vote, especially over the long run, is not necessarily accurate, it does provide an approximate near-term appraisal of value.

I know what you must be thinking. If the prices at which stocks trade in the market is a reasonable approximation of their value, then isn't this an admission that the stock market is efficient, the antithesis of one of the basic tenets of value investing? My answer is decidedly no. The stock market valuation of comparable businesses is but one of several valuation tools and provides a yardstick of what a security, if not a business, might bring if sold tomorrow.

Stock market value has its shortcomings as a valuation tool. You would not use stock market value to appraise each of the companies in an industry. It would be circular reasoning to observe that since newspaper companies tend to trade in the market at, say, eight times pretax cash flow, that is what they must be worth. Knowing the stock market's appraisal for the newspaper industry would be of some use, however, in estimating the near-term trading price of the newspaper subsidiary about to be spun off to the shareholders of a media conglomerate.

Choosing Among Valuation Methods

How should investors choose among these several valuation methods? When is one clearly preferable to the others? When one method yields very different values from the others, which should be trusted?

At times a particular method may stand out as the most appropriate. Net present value would be most applicable, for example, in valuing a high-return business with stable cash flows such as a consumer-products company; its liquidation value would be far too low. Similarly, a business with regulated rates of return on assets such as a utility might best be valued using NPV analysis. Liquidation analysis is probably the most appropriate method for valuing an unprofitable business whose stock trades well below book value. A closed-end fund or other company that owns only marketable securities should be valued by the stock market method; no other makes sense.

Often several valuation methods should be employed simultaneously. To value a complex entity such as a conglomerate operating several distinct businesses, for example, some portion of the assets might be best valued using one method and the rest with another. Frequently investors will want to use several methods to value a single business in order to obtain a range of values. In this case investors should err on the side of conservatism, adopting lower values over higher ones unless there is strong reason to do otherwise. True, conservatism may cause investors to refrain from making some investments that in hindsight would have been successful, but it will also prevent some sizable losses that would ensue from adopting less conservative business valuations.

The Reflexive Relationship Between Market Price and Underlying Value

A complicating factor in securities analysis is the reflexive or reciprocal relationship between security prices and the values of the underlying businesses. In *The Alchemy of Finance* George Soros stated, "Fundamental analysis seeks to establish how underlying values are reflected in stock prices, whereas the theory of reflexivity shows how stock prices can influence underlying values."[7] In other words, Soros's theory of reflexivity makes the point that its stock price can at times significantly influence the value of a business. Investors must not lose sight of this possibility.

Most businesses can exist indefinitely without concern for the prices of their securities as long as they have adequate capital. When additional capital is needed, however, the level of security prices can mean the difference between prosperity, mere viability, and bankruptcy. If, for example, an undercapitalized bank has a high stock price, it can issue more shares and become adequately capitalized, a form of self-fulfilling prophecy. The stock market says there is no problem, so there is no problem. In early 1991, for example, Citicorp stock traded in the teens and the company was able to find buyers for newly issued securities. If its stock price had been in the low single digits, however, it would have been unable to raise additional equity capital, which could have resulted in its eventual failure. This is another, albeit negative form of self-fulfilling prophecy, whereby the financial markets' perception of the viability of a business influences the outcome.

The same holds true for a highly leveraged company with an upcoming debt maturity. If the market deems a company creditworthy, as it did Marriott Corporation in early 1991, the company will be able to refinance and fulfill the prophecy. If the market votes thumbs down on the credit, however, as it did with Mortgage and Realty Trust in 1990, that prophecy will also be fulfilled since the company will then fail to meet its obligations.

Another form of reflexivity exists when the managers of a business accept its securities' prices, rather than business fundamentals, as the determining factor in valuation. If the management of a company with an undervalued stock believes that the depressed market price is an accurate reflection of value, they may take actions that prove the market right. Stock could be issued in a secondary offering or merger, for example, at a price so low that it significantly dilutes the value of existing shares.

As another example of reflexivity, the success of a reorganization plan for a bankrupt company may depend on certain values being realized by creditors. If the financial markets are depressed at the time of reorganization, it could be difficult, perhaps impossible, to generate agreed values for creditors if those values depend on the estimated market prices of debt and equity securities in the reorganized company. In circular fashion, this could serve to depress even further the prices of securities in this bankrupt company.

Reflexivity is a minor factor in the valuation of most securities most of the time, but occasionally it becomes important. This phenomenon is a wild card, a valuation factor not determined by business fundamentals but rather by the financial markets themselves.

Esco Electronics: An Exercise in Securities Valuation

Let me offer a specific example of the security valuation process. Esco Electronics Corporation is a defense company that was spun off[8] from Emerson Electric Company in October 1990; the shares were distributed free to shareholders of Emerson. Esco competes in a variety of defense-related businesses, including electronics, armaments, test equipment, and mobile tactical systems. Holders of Emerson received Esco shares on a one-for-twenty basis; that is, a holder of one thousand Emerson shares received fifty shares of Esco. Esco first traded at around $5 per share and quickly declined to $3; the spinoff valued at market prices was worth only fifteen cents per Emerson share (which itself traded around $40). Needless to say, many holders of Emerson quickly sold their trivial Esco holdings.

What was Esco worth at the time of spinoff? Was it undervalued in the marketplace, and if so, why? Was it an attractive value-investment opportunity? The way to answer these questions is to evaluate Esco using each of the methods that value investors employ.

To begin with, Esco is a substantial company, having approximately $500 million in annual sales and six thousand employees, who occupy 3.2 million square feet of space, 1.7 million of which are owned by the company. Esco's only recent growth has come from its acquisition of Hazeltine Corporation in late 1986 for $190 million (over $15 per Esco share). A major consideration leading to the spinoff was that Esco's after-tax profits had declined from $36.3 million in 1985 (actual) to $6.7 million (pro forma, to reflect adjustments related to the spinoff) in 1989 after $8.2 million of nonrecurring charges and to a loss of $5.2 million (pro forma) in 1990 after $13.8 million of nonrecurring charges. The company was spun off with a conservative capitalization, having only $45 million in debt compared with almost $500 million in equity. Tangible book value exceeded $25 per share, and net-net working capital, current assets less all liabilities, exceeded $15 per share.

Two questions regarding Esco's future worried investors. One was whether the sharp recent drop in profitability, related to money-losing defense contracts the company had taken on, would reverse. The second concerned the outcome of two pending contract disputes between Esco and the U.S. government; an adverse outcome could have cost Esco tens of millions of dollars in cash and forced it to report sizable losses. These uncertainties caused Emerson to spin off, not shares of common stock, but common stock trust receipts held in escrow in order to ensure that Esco would meet its obligation to indemnify Emerson for certain customer-contract guarantees.

The first step in valuing Esco in October 1990 was to try to understand its business results: earnings and cash flow. Esco's future earnings were particularly difficult to forecast, especially because in each of the preceding two years the company had taken significant nonrecurring charges. An analyst at Bear Stearns estimated break-even earnings for fiscal year 1991. This estimate was after the deduction of a newly instituted charge of $7.4 million, payable by Esco to Emerson each year from 1991 to 1995, for guaranteeing outstanding defense contracts. Although this charge would have the effect of reducing reported earnings for five years, it was not a true business expense but rather more of an extraordinary item.[9]

Another ongoing depressant to earnings was Esco's approximately $5 million per year charge for nondeductible goodwill amortization resulting from the Hazeltine acquisition. Since goodwill is a noncash expense, free cash flow from this source alone was $5 million, or forty-five cents per share.

In order to value Esco using NPV analysis, investors would need to forecast Esco's likely future cash flows. Goodwill amortization of forty-five cents a year, as stated, was free cash. Beginning in 1996 there would be an additional forty-five cents of after-tax earnings per year as the $7.4 million guaranty fee ended. Investors would have to make some assumptions regarding future earnings. One reasonable assumption, perhaps the most likely case, was that earnings, currently zero, would gradually increase over time. Unprofitable contracts would eventually be completed, and interest would be earned on accumulated cash flow. An alternative possibility was that results would remain at current depressed levels indefinitely.

In addition to predicting future earnings, investors would also need to estimate Esco's future cash investment or disinvestment in its business in order to assess its cash flow. Depreciation in recent years had approximated capital spending, for example, and assuming it would do so in the future seemed a conservative assumption. Also, working capital tied up in currently unprofitable contracts would eventually be freed for other corporate uses, but the timing of this was uncertain. Were Esco's working capital-to-sales ratio, currently bloated, to move into line with that of comparable defense electronics firms, roughly $80 million in additional cash would become available. To ensure conservatism, however, I chose to project no free cash flow from this source.

What was Esco worth if it never did better than its current depressed level of results? Cash flow would equal forty-five cents per share for five years and ninety cents thereafter when the guaranty payments to Emerson had ceased. The present value of these cash flows is $5.87 and $4.70 per share, calculated at 12 percent and 15 percent discount rates, respectively, which themselves reflect considerable uncertainty. If cash flow proved to be higher, the value would, of course, be greater.

What if Esco managed to increase its free cash flow by just $2.2 million a year, or twenty cents per share, for the next ten years, after which it leveled off? The present value of these flows at 12 percent and 15 percent discount rates is $14.76 and $10.83, respectively. Depending on the assumptions, then, the net present value per share of Esco is conservatively calculated at $4.70 and less pessimistically at $14.76 per share, clearly a wide range but in either case well above the $3 stock price and in no case making highly optimistic assumptions.

Investors in Esco would certainly want to consider alternative scenarios for future operating results. Obviously there was some chance that the company would lose one or more of its contract disputes with the U.S. government. There was some possibility that a widely anticipated reduction in national defense spending would cause the company to lose profitable contracts or fail to receive new ones. There was a chance that the newly independent company, smaller than most of its competitors, would face difficulties in trying to operate apart from Emerson.

Alternatively, there was some prospect that Esco would either win both of its contract disputes outright or settle with the government on acceptable terms. Indeed, the new top management would likely wish to start afresh, putting past difficulties behind them. (The disputes were, in fact, tentatively settled within months of the spinoff on terms favorable to Esco.) Further, new management expressed its intention to maximize cash flow rather than sales; new contracts would be accepted on the basis of low-risk profitability rather than prestige or the desire to achieve revenue growth. Thus it was not unreasonable to think that earnings would grow over time as unprofitable contracts were concluded and profitable contracts added.

Investors would want to consider other valuation methods in addition to NPV. The private-market value method, however, was not applicable in the case of Esco because there had been few recent business transactions involving sizable defense companies. Even if there had been, Esco's pending contract disputes would put a damper on anyone's enthusiasm to buy all of Esco except at an extreme bargain price. Indeed Esco had been put up for sale prior to spinoff, and no buyers emerged at prices acceptable to Emerson.

Conversely Emerson had only four years earlier paid $190 million for Hazeltine, which comprised only a fraction of Esco's business at the time of spinoff. At a takeover multiple even close to that of the Hazeltine transaction, all of Esco would be worth many times its prevailing stock market price, with Hazeltine alone worth $15 per Esco share.

A liquidation analysis was also not particularly applicable; defense companies cannot be easily liquidated. The assets have few alternate uses, and inventory and receivable valuations are realizable only for an ongoing defense concern. Esco could be valued, however, on the basis of a gradual liquidation, whereby existing contracts would be allowed to run to completion and no new business would be sought. The value in such a scenario is uncertain, but it is hard to imagine the proceeds realized over time being less than the net-net working capital of $15 per share.

Stock market value is another useful yardstick, especially for gauging where a spinoff new to the market might reasonably be expected to trade. This method would not determine over- or undervaluation, but simply relative valuation compared with other defense-electronics companies. In this case Esco seemed to trade as if its business were located on a different planet. At $3 per share, the stock sold for only 12 percent of tangible book

value, a staggeringly low level for a viable company with positive cash flow and little debt. Indeed, the shares could rise 400
percent from that level and still be below half of tangible book
value. Of course, other defense company shares were also
depressed at the time, with most of them trading at only four to
six times earnings; another recent defense spinoff, Alliant
Techsystems, traded at only two times estimated earnings.
However, most comparable firms were trading at between 60
and 100 percent of book value and had historically traded considerably above that. Although Esco was less profitable than
most other defense companies, it was selling for only three
times earnings if both goodwill amortization and the $7.4 mil-
lion special charge were ignored. The extremely low valuation
seemed to more than fully discount Esco's current shortcomings
as a business.

It is difficult, if not impossible, to determine precisely what
Esco stock was worth. It is far simpler to determine that it was
worth considerably more than the market price. With the shares
selling for $3, yet having $25 per share of tangible book value
and little debt, investors' margin of safety was high.

Esco appeared to be worth easily twice its $3 market price, a
level that was only six times adjusted earnings, 40 percent of
net-net working capital, and less than 25 percent of tangible
book value. Was it worth $10 per share? Probably, either on the
basis of NPV using mildly optimistic assumptions or on a gradual liquidation basis.

The nice thing about Esco at $3 per share is that one didn't
have to know exactly what it was worth. The price reflected dis-
aster; any other outcome seemed certain to yield a higher price.
A sizable loss on the disputed contracts was the worst-case scenario, but even that was probably already reflected in the low
share price. Management certainly believed that these disputes
could be favorably resolved. According to public filings, shortly
after the spinoff the chairman of Esco's board purchased shares
on the open market for his personal account. By early 1991 selling pressure related to the spinoff subsided, defense stocks ral-
lied, and Esco rose to over $8 per share.

Conventional Valuation Yardsticks: Earnings, Book Value, and Dividend Yield

Earnings and Earnings Growth

We are near the end of a chapter on business valuation, and there has been virtually no mention of earnings, book value, or dividend yield. Both earnings and book value have a place in securities analysis but must be used with caution and as part of a more comprehensive valuation effort.

Earnings per share has historically been the valuation yardstick most commonly used by investors. Unfortunately, as we shall see, it is an imprecise measure, subject to manipulation and accounting vagaries. It does not attempt to measure the cash generated or used by a business. And as with any prediction of the future, earnings are nearly impossible to forecast.

Corporate managements are generally aware that many investors focus on growth in reported earnings, and a number of them gently massage reported earnings to create a consistent upward trend. A few particularly unscrupulous managements play accounting games to turn deteriorating results into improving ones, losses into profits, and small profits into large ones.

Even without manipulation, analysis of reported earnings can mislead investors as to the real profitability of a business. Generally accepted accounting practices (GAAP) may require actions that do not reflect business reality. By way of example, amortization of goodwill, a noncash charge required under GAAP, can artificially depress reported earnings; an analysis of cash flow would better capture the true economics of a business. By contrast, nonrecurring gains can boost earnings to unsustainable levels, and should be ignored by investors.[10]

Most important, whether investors use earnings or cash flow in their valuation analysis, it is important to remember that the numbers are not an end in themselves. Rather they are a means to understanding what is really happening in a company.

Book Value

What something cost in the past is not necessarily a good measure of its value today. Book value is the historical accounting of shareholders' equity, the residual after liabilities are subtracted from assets. Sometimes historical book value (carrying value) provides an accurate measure of current value, but often it is way off the mark. Current assets, such as receivables and inventories, for example, are usually worth close to carrying value, although certain types of inventory are subject to rapid obsolescence. Plant and equipment, however, may be outmoded or obsolete and therefore worth considerably less than carrying value. Alternatively, a company with fully depreciated plant and equipment or a history of write-offs may have carrying value considerably below real economic value.

Inflation, technological change, and regulation, among other factors, can affect the value of assets in ways that historical cost accounting cannot capture. Real estate purchased decades ago, for example, and carried on a company's books at historical cost may be worth considerably more. The cost of building a new oil refinery today may be made prohibitively expensive by environmental legislation, endowing older facilities with a scarcity value. Aging integrated steel facilities, by contrast, may be technologically outmoded compared with newly built minimills. As a result, their book value may be significantly overstated.

Reported book value can also be affected by management actions. Write-offs of money-losing operations are somewhat arbitrary yet can have a large impact on reported book value. Share issuance and repurchases can also affect book value. Many companies in the 1980s, for example, performed recapitalizations, whereby money was borrowed and distributed to shareholders as an extraordinary dividend. This served to greatly reduce the book value of these companies, sometimes below zero. Even the choice of accounting method for mergers—purchase or pooling of interests—can affect reported book value.

To be useful, an analytical tool must be consistent in its valuations. Yet, as a result of accounting rules and discretionary management actions, two companies with identical tangible assets and liabilities could have very different reported book values. This renders book value not terribly useful as a valuation yardstick. As with earnings, book value provides limited information to investors and should only be considered as one component of a more thorough and complete analysis.

Dividend Yield

Why is my discussion of dividend yield so short? Although at one time a measure of a business's prosperity, it has become a relic: stocks should simply not be bought on the basis of their dividend yield. Too often struggling companies sport high dividend yields, not because the dividends have been increased, but because the share prices have fallen. Fearing that the stock price will drop further if the dividend is cut, managements maintain the payout, weakening the company even more. Investors buying such stocks for their ostensibly high yields may not be receiving good value. On the contrary, they may be the victims of a pathetic manipulation. The high dividend paid by such companies is not a return on invested capital but rather a return of capital that represents the liquidation of the underlying business. This manipulation was widely used by money-center banks through most of the 1980s and had the (desired) effect of propping up their share prices.

Conclusion

Business valuation is a complex process yielding imprecise and uncertain results. Many businesses are so diverse or difficult to understand that they simply cannot be valued. Some investors willingly voyage into the unknown and buy into such businesses, impatient with the discipline required by value investing. Investors must remember that they need not swing at every pitch to do well over time; indeed, selectivity undoubtedly improves an investor's results. For every business that cannot be valued, there are many others that can. Investors who confine themselves to what they know, as difficult as that may be, have a considerable advantage over everyone else.

Notes

1. Benjamin Graham and David L. Dodd, in Charles D. Ellis and James R. Vertin, eds., *Classics: An Investor's Anthology* (Homewood, Ill.: Dow Jones-Irwin, 1989), p. 50.
2. Some investors value businesses by discounting earnings rather than cash flow. For some businesses, such as banks and thrifts, earnings approximate cash flow and may be used instead. In most cases, however, cash flow is the appropriate valuation yardstick. The calculation of cash flow is discussed at length in chapter 4.
3. Managements not only respond to uncertainty; they sometimes enhance it by taking unpredictable or ill-considered actions.
4. See William A. Sahlman (Harvard Graduate School of Business Administration Case Study, June 1990), "A Cautionary Tale about Discounted Cash Flow Analysis," for a superb discussion of the difficulties of generating useful valuations from discounted cash flow analysis.
5. Berkshire Hathaway, Inc., annual report for 1982, p. 5.
6. There is considerable academic debate concerning whether short-term or long-term interest rates should be applied. My view is to match the timing of the cash flows to the maturity of the U.S. Treasury security.
7. George Soros, *The Alchemy of Finance* (New York: Simon & Schuster, 1987), p. 51.
8. A discussion of the opportunity for investors in corporate spinoffs can be found in chapter 10.
9. Had the same flow of cash from Esco to Emerson been structured as an interest-bearing note payable, for example, the same $7.4 million annual payment would have had less than half the impact on reported earnings. In that case, much of the $7.4 million payment would have represented repayment of principal, which is not an expense.

10. While cash flow is less distorted by accounting quirks than earnings, it too can be manipulated if a company is so inclined. Cash flow can be temporarily increased, for example, by a reduction in capital spending; however, this eventually leads to deterioration of the business.

III

THE VALUE-
INVESTMENT PROCESS

9

Investment Research: The Challenge of Finding Attractive Investments

While knowing how to value businesses is essential for investment success, the first and perhaps most important step in the investment process is knowing where to look for opportunities. Investors are in the business of processing information, but while studying the current financial statements of the thousands of publicly held companies, the monthly, weekly, and even daily research reports of hundreds of Wall Street analysts, and the market behavior of scores of stocks and bonds, they will spend virtually all their time reviewing fairly priced securities that are of no special interest.

Good investment ideas are rare and valuable things, which must be ferreted out assiduously. They do not fly in over the transom or materialize out of thin air. Investors cannot assume that good ideas will come effortlessly from scanning the recommendations of Wall Street analysts, no matter how highly regarded, or from punching up computers, no matter how cleverly programmed, although both can sometimes indicate interesting places to hunt.

Upon occasion attractive opportunities are so numerous that the only limiting factor is the availability of funds to invest; typically the number of attractive opportunities is much more limited. By identifying where the most attractive opportunities are likely to arise before starting one's quest for the exciting handful of specific investments, investors can spare themselves an often fruitless survey of the humdrum majority of available investments.

Value investing encompasses a number of specialized investment niches that can be divided into three categories: securities selling at a discount to breakup or liquidation value, rate-of-return situations, and asset-conversion opportunities. Where to look for opportunities varies from one of these categories to the next.

Computer-screening techniques, for example, can be helpful in identifying stocks of the first category: those selling at a discount from liquidation value. Because databases can be out of date or inaccurate, however, it is essential that investors verify that the computer output is correct.

Risk arbitrage and complex securities comprise a second category of attractive value investments with known exit prices and approximate time frames, which, taken together, enable investors to calculate expected rates of return at the time the investments are made. Mergers, tender offers, and other risk-arbitrage transactions are widely reported in the daily financial press—the *Wall Street Journal* and the business section of the *New York Times*—as well as in specialized newsletters and periodicals. Locating information on complex securities is more difficult, but as they often come into existence as byproducts of risk arbitrage transactions, investors who follow the latter may become aware of the former.

Financially distressed and bankrupt securities, corporate recapitalizations, and exchange offers all fall into the category of asset conversions, in which investors' existing holdings are exchanged for one or more new securities. Distressed and bankrupt businesses are often identified in the financial press; specialized publications and research services also provide information on such companies and their securities. Fundamental information on troubled companies can be gleaned from published financial statements and in the case of bankruptcies, from court documents. Price quotations may only be available from dealers since many of these securities are not listed on any exchange. Corporate recapitalizations and exchange offers can usually be identified from a close reading of the daily financial press. Publicly available filings with the Securities and Exchange Commission (SEC) provide extensive detail on these extraordinary corporate transactions.

Many undervalued securities do not fall into any of these specialized categories and are best identified through old-fashioned hard work, yet there are widely available means of improving the likelihood of finding mispriced securities. Looking at stocks on the *Wall Street Journal*'s leading percentage-decline and new-low lists, for example, occasionally turns up an out-of-favor investment idea. Similarly, when a company eliminates its dividend, its shares often fall to unduly depressed levels. Of course, all companies of requisite size produce annual and quarterly reports, which they will send upon request. Filings of a company's annual and quarterly financial statements on Forms 10K and 10Q, respectively, are available from the SEC and often from the reporting company as well.

Sometimes an attractive investment niche emerges in which numerous opportunities develop over time. One such area has been the large number of thrift institutions that have converted from mutual to stock ownership (see chapter 11). Investors should consider analyzing all companies within such a category in order to identify those that are undervalued. Specialized newsletters and industry periodicals can be excellent sources of information on such niche opportunities.

Market Inefficiencies and Institutional Constraints

The research task does not end with the discovery of an apparent bargain. It is incumbent on investors to try to find out why the bargain has become available. If in 1990 you were looking for an ordinary, four-bedroom colonial home on a quarter acre in the Boston suburbs, you should have been prepared to pay at least $300,000. If you learned of one available for $150,000, your first reaction would not have been, "What a great bargain!" but, "What's wrong with it?"

The same healthy skepticism applies to the stock market. A bargain should be inspected and reinspected for possible flaws. Irrational or indifferent selling alone may have made it cheap, but there may be more fundamental reasons for the depressed price. Perhaps there are contingent liabilities or pending litigation that you are unaware of. Maybe a competitor is preparing to introduce a superior product.

When the reason for the undervaluation can be clearly identified, it becomes an even better investment because the outcome is more predictable. By way of example, the legal constraint that prevents some institutional investors from purchasing low-priced spinoffs (see chapter 10) is one possible explanation for undervaluation. Such reasons give investors some comfort that the price is not depressed for an undisclosed fundamental business reason.

Other institutional constraints can also create opportunities for value investors. For example, many institutional investors become major sellers of securities involved in risk-arbitrage transactions on the grounds that their mission is to invest in ongoing businesses, not speculate on takeovers. The resultant selling pressure can depress prices, increasing the returns available to arbitrage investors.

Institutional investors are commonly unwilling to buy or hold low-priced securities. Since any company can exercise a degree of control over its share price through splitting or reverse-splitting its outstanding shares, the financial rationale for this constraint is hard to understand. Why would a company's shares be a good buy at $15 a share but not at $3 after a five-for-one stock split or vice versa?

Many attractive investment opportunities result from market inefficiencies, that is, areas of the security markets in which information is not fully disseminated or in which supply and demand are temporarily out of balance. Almost no one on Wall Street, for example, follows, let alone recommends, small companies whose shares are closely held and infrequently traded; there are at most a handful of market makers in such stocks. Depending on the number of shareholders, such companies may not even be required by the SEC to file quarterly or annual reports. Obscurity and a very thin market can cause stocks to sell at depressed levels.

Year-end tax selling also creates market inefficiencies. The Internal Revenue Code makes it attractive for investors to realize capital losses before the end of each year. Selling driven by the calendar rather than by investment fundamentals frequently causes stocks that declined significantly during the year to decline still further. This generates opportunities for value investors.

Value Investing and Contrarian Thinking

Value investing by its very nature is contrarian. Out-of-favor securities may be undervalued; popular securities almost never are. What the herd is buying is, by definition, in favor. Securities in favor have already been bid up in price on the basis of optimistic expectations and are unlikely to represent good value that has been overlooked.

If value is not likely to exist in what the herd is buying, where may it exist? In what they are selling, unaware of, or ignoring. When the herd is selling a security, the market price may fall well beyond reason. Ignored, obscure, or newly created securities may similarly be or become undervalued.

Investors may find it difficult to act as contrarians for they can never be certain whether or when they will be proven correct. Since they are acting against the crowd, contrarians are almost always initially wrong and likely for a time to suffer paper losses. By contrast, members of the herd are nearly always right for a period. Not only are contrarians initially wrong, they may be wrong more often and for longer periods than others because market trends can continue long past any limits warranted by underlying value.

Holding a contrary opinion is not always useful to investors, however. When widely held opinions have no influence on the issue at hand, nothing is gained by swimming against the tide. It is always the consensus that the sun will rise tomorrow, but this view does not influence the outcome. By contrast, when majority opinion does affect the outcome or the odds, contrary opinion can be put to use. When the herd rushes into home health-care stocks, bidding up prices and thereby lowering available returns, the majority has altered the risk/reward ratio, allowing contrarians to bet against the crowd with the odds skewed in their favor. When investors in 1983 either ignored or panned the stock of Nabisco, causing it to trade at a discount to other food companies, the risk/reward ratio became more favorable, creating a buying opportunity for contrarians.

How Much Research and Analysis Are Sufficient?

Some investors insist on trying to obtain perfect knowledge about their impending investments, researching companies until they think they know everything there is to know about them. They study the industry and the competition, contact for-mer employees, industry consultants, and analysts, and become personally acquainted with top management. They analyze financial statements for the past decade and stock price trends for even longer. This diligence is admirable, but it has two shortcomings. First, no matter how much research is performed, some information always remains elusive; investors have to learn to live with less than complete information. Second, even if an investor could know all the facts about an investment, he or she would not necessarily profit.

This is not to say that fundamental analysis is not useful. It certainly is. But information generally follows the well-known

80/20 rule: the first 80 percent of the available information is gathered in the first 20 percent of the time spent. The value of in-depth fundamental analysis is subject to diminishing marginal returns.

Information is not always easy to obtain. Some companies actually impede its flow. Understandably, proprietary information must be kept confidential. The requirement that all investors be kept on an equal footing is another reason for the limited dissemination of information; information limited to a privileged few might be construed as inside information. Restrictions on the dissemination of information can complicate investors' quest for knowledge nevertheless.

Moreover, business information is highly perishable. Economic conditions change, industries are transformed, and business results are volatile. The effort to acquire current, let alone complete information is never-ending. Meanwhile, other market participants are also gathering and updating information, thereby diminishing any investor's informational advantage.

David Dreman recounts "the story of an analyst so knowledgeable about Clorox that 'he could recite bleach shares by brand in every small town in the Southwest and tell you the production levels of Clorox's line number 2, plant number 3. But somehow, when the company began to develop massive problems, he missed the signs. . . .' The stock fell from a high of 53 to 11."[1]

Although many Wall Street analysts have excellent insight into industries and individual companies, the results of investors who follow their recommendations may be less than stellar. In part this is due to the pressure placed on these analysts to recommend frequently rather than wisely, but it also exemplifies the difficulty of translating information into profits. Industry analysts are not well positioned to evaluate the stocks they follow in the context of competing investment alternatives. Merrill Lynch's pharmaceutical analyst may know everything there is to know about Merck and Pfizer, but he or she knows virtually nothing about General Motors, Treasury bond yields, and Jones & Laughlin Steel first-mortgage bonds.

Most investors strive fruitlessly for certainty and precision, avoiding situations in which information is difficult to obtain. Yet high uncertainty is frequently accompanied by low prices. By the time the uncertainty is resolved, prices are likely to have risen. Investors frequently benefit from making investment decisions with less than perfect knowledge and are well rewarded for bearing the risk of uncertainty. The time other investors spend delving into the last unanswered detail may cost them the chance to buy in at prices so low that they offer a margin of safety despite the incomplete information.

Insider Buying and Management Stock Options Can Signal Opportunity

In their search for complete information on businesses, investors often overlook one very important clue. In most instances no one understands a business and its prospects better than the management. Therefore investors should be encouraged when corporate insiders invest their own money alongside that of shareholders by purchasing stock in the open market. It is often said on Wall Street that there are many reasons why an insider might sell a stock (need for cash to pay taxes, expenses, etc.), but there is only one reason for buying. Investors can track insider buying and selling in any of several specialized publications, such as *Vickers Stock Research*.

The motivation of corporate management can be a very important force in determining the outcome of an investment. Some companies provide incentives for their managements with stock-option plans and related vehicles. Usually these plans give management the specific incentive to do what they can to boost the company's share price.

While management does not control a company's stock price, it can greatly influence the gap between share price and underlying value and over time can have a significant influence on value itself. If the management of a company were compensated based on revenues, total assets, or even net income, it might ignore share price while focusing on those indicators of corporate performance. If, however, management were provided incentives to maximize share price, it would focus its attention differently. For example, the management of a company whose stock sold at $25 with an underlying value of $50 could almost certainly boost the market price by announcing a spinoff, recapitalization, or asset sale, with the result of narrowing the gap between share price and underlying value. The repurchase of shares on the open market at $25 would likely give a boost to the share price as well as causing the underlying value of remaining shares to increase above $50. Obviously investors need to be alert to the motivations of managements at the companies in which they invest.

Investment Research and Inside Information

The investment research process is complicated by the blurred line between publicly available and inside, or privileged, information. Although trading based on inside information is illegal, the term has never been clearly defined. As investors seek to analyze investments and value securities, they bump into the unresolved question of how far they may reasonably go in the pursuit of information. For example, can an investor presume that information provided by a corporate executive is public knowledge (assuming, of course, that suitcases of money do not change hands)? Similarly, is information that emanates from a stockbroker in the public domain? How about information from investment bankers? If not the latter, then why do investors risk talking to them, and why are the investment bankers willing to speak?

How far may investors go in conducting fundamental research? How deep may they dig? May they hire private investigators, and may those investigators comb through a company's garbage? What, if any, are the limits?

Do different rules apply to equities than to other securities?

The troubled debt market, for example, is event driven. Takeovers, exchange offers, and open-market bond repurchases are fairly routine. What is public knowledge, and what is not? If you sell bonds back to a company, which then retires them, is knowledge of that trade inside information? Does it matter how many bonds were sold or when the trade occurred? If this constitutes inside information, in what way does it restrict you? If you are a large bondholder and the issuer contacts you to discuss an exchange offer, in what way can that be construed as inside information?

When does inside information become sufficiently old to no longer be protected? When do internal financial projections become outdated? When do aborted merger plans cease to be secret?

There are no firm answers to these questions. Investors must bend over backward to stay within the law, of course, but it would be far easier if the law were more clearly enunciated. Since it is not, law abiding investors must err on the side of ignorance, investing with less information than those who are not so ethical. When investors are unsure whether they have crossed the line, they would be well advised to ask their sources and perhaps their attorneys as well before making any trades.

Conclusion

Investment research is the process of reducing large piles of information to manageable ones, distilling the investment wheat from the chaff. There is, needless to say, a lot of chaff and very little wheat. The research process itself, like the factory of a manufacturing company, produces no profits. The profits materialize later, often much later, when the undervaluation identified during the research process is first translated into portfolio decisions and then eventually recognized by the market. In fact, often there is no immediate buying opportunity; today's research may be advance preparation for tomorrow's opportunities. In any event, just as a superior sales force cannot succeed if the factory does not produce quality goods, an investment program will not long succeed if high-quality research is not performed on a continuing basis.

Notes

1. Charles D. Ellis and James R. Vertin, eds., *Classics: An Investor's Anthology* (Homewood, Ill.: Dow Jones-Irwin, 1989), p. 513.

10

Areas of Opportunity for Value Investors: Catalysts, Market Inefficiencies, and Institutional Constraints

The attraction of some value investments is simple and straightforward: ongoing, profitable, and growing businesses with share prices considerably below conservatively appraised underlying value. Ordinarily, however, the simpler the analysis and steeper the discount, the more obvious the bargain becomes to other investors. The securities of high-return businesses therefore reach compelling levels of undervaluation only infrequently. Usually investors have to work harder and dig deeper to find undervalued opportunities, either by ferreting out hidden value or by comprehending a complex situation.

Once a security is purchased at a discount from underlying value, shareholders can benefit immediately if the stock price rises to better reflect underlying value or if an event occurs that causes that value to be realized by shareholders. Such an event eliminates investors' dependence on market forces for investment profits. By precipitating the realization of underlying value, moreover, such an event considerably enhances investors' margin of safety. I refer to such events as catalysts.

Some catalysts for the realization of underlying value exist at the discretion of a company's management and board of directors. The decision to sell out or liquidate, for example, is made internally. Other catalysts are external and often relate to the voting control of a company's stock. Control of the majority of a company's stock typically allows the holder to elect the majority of the board of directors. Thus accumulation of stock leading to voting control, or simply management's fear that this might happen, could lead to steps being taken by a company that cause its share price to more fully reflect underlying value.

Catalysts vary in their potency. The orderly sale or liquidation of a business leads to total value realization. Corporate spinoffs, share buybacks, recapitalizations, and major asset sales usually bring about only partial value realization.

The emergence of a company from bankruptcy serves as a catalyst for creditors. Holders of senior debt securities, for example, typically receive cash, debt instruments, and/or equity securities in the reorganized entity in satisfaction of their claims. The total market value of these distributions is likely to be higher than the market value of the bankrupt debt; securities in the reorganized company will typically be more liquid and avoid most of the stigma and uncertainty of bankruptcy and thus trade at higher multiples. Moreover, committees of creditors will have participated in determining the capital structure of the reorganized firm, seeking to create a structure that maximizes market value.

Value investors are always on the lookout for catalysts. While buying assets at a discount from underlying value is the defining characteristic of value investing, the partial or total realization of underlying value through a catalyst is an important means of generating profits. Furthermore, the presence of a catalyst serves to reduce risk. If the gap between price and underlying value is likely to be closed quickly, the probability of losing money due to market fluctuations or adverse business developments is reduced. In the absence of a catalyst, however, underlying value could erode; conversely, the gap between price and value could widen with the vagaries of the market. Owning securities with catalysts for value realization is therefore an important way for investors to reduce the risk within their portfolios, augmenting the margin of safety achieved by investing at a discount from underlying value.

Catalysts that bring about total value realization are, of course, optimal. Nevertheless, catalysts for partial value realization serve two important purposes. First, they do help to realize underlying value, sometimes by placing it directly into the hands of shareholders such as through a recapitalization or spinoff and other times by reducing the discount between price and underlying value, such as through a share buyback. Second, a company that takes action resulting in the partial realization of underlying value for shareholders serves notice that management is shareholder oriented and may pursue additional value-realization strategies in the future. Over the years, for example, investors in Teledyne have repeatedly benefitted from timely share repurchases and spinoffs.

Investing in Corporate Liquidations

Some troubled companies, lacking viable alternatives, voluntarily liquidate in order to preempt a total wipeout of shareholders' investments. Other, more interesting corporate liquidations are motivated by tax considerations, persistent stock market undervaluation, or the desire to escape the grasp of a corporate raider. A company involved in only one profitable line of business would typically prefer selling out to liquidating because possible double taxation (taxes both at the corporate and shareholder level) would be avoided. A company operating in diverse business lines, however, might find a liquidation or breakup to be the value-maximizing alternative, particularly if the liquidation process triggers a loss that results in a tax refund. Some of the most attractive corporate liquidations in the past decade have involved the breakup of conglomerates and investment companies.

Most equity investors prefer (or are effectively required) to hold shares in ongoing businesses. Companies in liquidation are the antithesis of the type of investment they want to make. Even some risk arbitrageurs (who have been known to buy just about anything) avoid investing in liquidations, believing the process to be too uncertain or protracted. Indeed, investing in liquidations is sometimes disparagingly referred to as cigar-butt investing, whereby an investor picks up someone else's discard with a few puffs left on it and smokes it. Needless to say, because other investors disparage and avoid them, corporate liquidations may be particularly attractive opportunities for value investors.

City Investing Liquidating Trust

In 1984 shareholders of City Investing Company voted to liquidate. The assets of this conglomerate were diverse, and the most valuable subsidiary, Home Insurance Company, was particularly difficult for investors to appraise. Efforts to sell Home Insurance failed, and it was instead spun off to City Investing shareholders. The remaining assets were put into a newly formed entity called City Investing Liquidating Trust, which became a wonderful investment opportunity.

Table 2

**Assets of City Investing Liquidating Trust at Its Inception,
September 25, 1985**

Assets	Estimated value ($ in millions)	Derivation of value
$9 million cash	$ 9.0	cash value
General Development Corp. common stock and warrants	46.0	market price
7.3 million shares Pace Industries	36.5	cost
$55 million debentures Pace Group Holdings	40.0	estimated net present value
$17 million subordinated debt (Wood Brothers Homes)	9.0	estimate
$18 million Brazilian receivables ($10 million received to date not counted in cash)	12.0	estimate
$15 million miscellaneous notes and mortgages	10.0	estimate
$11 million miscellaneous investments	6.0	estimate
$35 million estimated federal income taxes recoverable	31.0	net present value
total assets	$199.5	
less known liabilities	4.0	
net assets	$195.5	
or	$ 5.02 per unit,	

exclusive of miscellaneous contingent liabilities

As shown in table 2, City Investing Liquidating Trust was a hodgepodge of assets. Few investors had the inclination or stamina to evaluate these assets or the willingness to own them for the duration of a liquidation likely to take several years. Thus, while the units were ignored by most potential buyers, they sold in high volume at approximately $3, or substantially below underlying value.

The shares of City Investing Liquidating Trust traded initially at depressed levels for a number of additional reasons. Many investors in the liquidation of City Investing had been disappointed with the prices received for assets sold previously and with City's apparent inability to sell Home Insurance and complete its liquidation. Consequently many disgruntled investors in City Investing quickly dumped the liquidating trust units to move on to other opportunities. Once the intended spinoff of Home Insurance was announced, many investors purchased City Investing shares as a way of establishing an investment in Home Insurance before it began trading on its own, buying in at what they perceived to be a bargain price. Most of these investors were not interested in the liquidating trust, and sold their units upon receipt of the Home Insurance spinoff. In addition, the per unit market price of City Investing Liquidating Trust was below the minimum price threshold of many institutional investors. Since City Investing Company had been widely held by institutional investors, those who hadn't sold earlier became natural sellers of the liquidating trust due to the low market price. Finally, after the Home Insurance spinoff, City Investing Liquidating Trust was delisted from the New York Stock Exchange. Trading initially only in the over-the-counter pink-sheet market, the units had no ticker symbol. Quotes were unobtainable either on-line or in most newspapers. This prompted further selling while simultaneously discouraging potential buyers.

The calculation of City Investing Liquidating Trust's underlying value in table 2 is deliberately conservative. An important component of the eventual liquidating proceeds, and something investors mostly overlooked (a hidden value), was that City's investment in the stock of Pace Industries, Inc., was at the time almost certainly worth more than historical cost. Pace was a company formed by Kohlberg, Kravis and Roberts (KKR) to purchase the Rheem, Uarco, and World Color Press businesses of City Investing in a December 1984 leveraged buyout. This buyout was profitable and performing well nine months later when the City Investing Liquidating Trust was formed.

The businesses of Pace had been purchased by KKR from City Investing in a financial environment quite different from the one that existed in September 1985. The interest rate on U.S. government bonds had declined by several hundred basis points in the intervening nine months, and the major stock market indexes had spurted sharply higher. These changes had almost certainly increased the value of City's equity interest in Pace. This increased the apparent value of City Investing Liquidating Trust units well above the $5.02 estimate, making them an even more attractive bargain.

As with any value investment, the greater the undervaluation, the greater the margin of safety to investors. Moreover, approximately half of City's value was comprised of liquid assets and marketable securities, further reducing the risk of a serious decline in value. Investors could reduce risk even more if they chose by selling short publicly traded General Development Corporation (GDV) shares in an amount equal to the number of GDV shares underlying their investment in the trust in order to lock in the value of City's GDV holdings.

As it turned out, City Investing Liquidating Trust made rapid progress in liquidating. GDV shares surged in price and were distributed directly to unitholders. Wood Brothers Homes was sold, various receivables were collected, and most lucrative of all, City Investing received large cash distributions when Pace Industries sold its Rheem and Uarco subsidiaries at a substantial gain. The Pace Group debentures were redeemed prior to maturity with proceeds from the same asset sales. Meanwhile a number of the trust's contingent liabilities were extinguished at little or no cost. By 1991 investors who purchased City Investing Liquidating Trust at inception had received several liquidating distributions with a combined value of approximately nine dollars per unit, or three times the September 1985 market price, with much of the value received in the early years of the liquidation process.

Investing in Complex Securities

I define complex securities as those with unusual contractual cash flow characteristics. Unlike bonds, which provide a constant cash stream to investors, a complex security typically distributes cash according to some contingent event, such as the future achievement of a specified level of earnings, the price of a particular commodity, or the value of specified assets. Often brought into existence as a result of mergers or reorganizations, their inherent complexity falls outside the investment parameters and scope of most investors. Indeed, while some complex securities are stocks or bonds, many of them are neither. As a result of their obscurity and uniqueness, complex securities may offer to value investors unusually attractive returns for a given level of risk.

Complex securities have existed throughout modern financial history. In the 1930s, for example, railroad bankruptcies often resulted in the creation of income bonds, which paid interest only if the issuer attained certain levels of income. In 1958 the Missouri-Kansas-Texas Railroad Company (MKT) reorganized and issued participation certificates whose only entitlement to monetary benefit consisted of the right to have payments made into a sinking fund for their retirement. Such payments were required to be made only after accumulated earnings reached a specified level as defined in the indenture. The certificates traded for years in the illiquid pink sheet market at very low prices, partly as a result of investor neglect. In 1985 MKT was merged into the Missouri Pacific Railroad Company, and the certificates were the target of a tender offer at several times the market price prevailing earlier that year.

As another example of a complex security, when Bank-America Corporation acquired Seafirst Corporation in 1983, a series of preferred stock was issued as partial consideration to Seafirst shareholders. The dividend was fixed for five years and then would fluctuate based on prevailing market conditions. The redemption price could also be reset, based on the value of certain problem loans in Seafirst's portfolio. In effect, if losses exceeded $500 million on a specified $1.2 billion pool of troubled loans, the preferred stock with a $25 original par value would likely be retired by BankAmerica at only $2 per share. Since few investors understood how to value such an atypical security, from time to time its price dropped to levels that were attractive even on a worst-case basis.

Another example of a complex security was the contingent-value rights issued to Marion Laboratories, Inc., shareholders by Dow Chemical Company as part of the combination of Marion with Dow's Merrell Dow Pharmaceuticals, Inc., subsidiary in December 1989. Two or three years after their issuance (at Dow's option) these separately tradable rights would be redeemed for cash if Marion stock failed to reach designated levels. Specifically, the rights entitled holders to the difference on September 30, 1991, between $45.77 and the average Marion share price between June 19 and September 18, 1991, up to a maximum of $15.77 per right. In effect, these were put options on Marion stock which had a ceiling on their value. Dow Chemical owned roughly 67 percent of Marion Merrell Dow, Inc.; the public owned the remaining 92 million shares, as well as a similar number of contingent-value rights. The highly unusual nature of these securities ensured very limited demand from institutional and individual investors and increased the likelihood that they would at times become undervalued compared with other publicly traded options.

Not all complex securities are worthwhile investments. They may be overpriced or too difficult to evaluate. Nevertheless this area frequently is fertile ground for bargain hunting by value investors.

Investing in Rights Offerings

Rights offerings are more esoteric than many other investments and for this reason may occasionally be of interest to value investors. Some rights offerings present attractive bargains, but many are fully priced or even overpriced. Investors may find this an interesting area to examine but as usual must do their homework.

Unlike a typical underwritten share offering, where buying

by new investors dilutes the percentage interest of current shareholders, in a rights offering shareholders are given the opportunity to preserve their proportional interest in the issuer by subscribing for additional shares. Those who subscribe retain the same percentage interest in the business but have more of their money at stake. Investors who fail to exercise their rights often leave money on the table, creating an opportunity for alert value investors.

Rights offerings can effectively compel current shareholders to put up more money in order to avoid considerable dilution of their investments. By way of example, assume XYZ is a closed-end mutual fund with one million shares outstanding, which trade at a price equal to the fund's net asset value of $25. Further assume that XYZ, seeking to raise an additional $15 million to take advantage of market opportunities, issues every holder a nontransferable right to buy another XYZ share for $15. If all holders subscribe, then immediately after the rights offering XYZ will have two million shares outstanding and $40 million of total assets, or $20 per share. If holders of 50,000 shares do not exercise their rights, while holders of 950,000 shares do, the 1,950,000 shares outstanding after the rights offering will have a net asset value of $20.13. The investors who subscribed will have an average cost of $20 per share, while those who did not will have an average cost of $25. Since nonsubscribers will suffer an immediate loss of almost 20 percent of their underlying value, all holders have a powerful incentive to subscribe.

Some rights offerings give holders the opportunity to oversubscribe beyond their own proportional interest for shares that others do not buy. In the case of XYZ, investors who chose to oversubscribe for the 50,000 shares left unsold at the original offering could have made a quick $250,000 buying those shares at $15 and promptly selling them at the pro forma net asset value of $20.

Companies occasionally employ a rights offering to effectuate the initial public offering of shares in a subsidiary. In 1984, for example, Consolidated Oil and Gas, Inc., utilized a rights offering to bring its Princeville Development Corporation subsidiary public. Consolidated was an overleveraged energy company that owned some attractive Hawaiian real estate properties, which were held by its Princeville subsidiary. To separate the Hawaiian properties from the rest of the business while preserving the value of those properties in shareholders' hands, Consolidated conducted a rights offering. Under its terms shareholders of Consolidated were offered the right to purchase one share of Princeville for each share of Consolidated they owned. The initial offering price, $3.25 per share, was arbitrary, according to the prospectus, and considerably below Consolidated's cost basis in Princeville.

When the rights started to trade, little information had been released by Consolidated Oil and Gas concerning Princeville. The prospectus was apparently not yet publicly available. In the absence of publicly available information, some rights traded for as little as 1/32 and 1/64 of a dollar per right. Alert investors willing to make an educated guess were able to earn an enormous profit on this obscure rights offering; upon completion of the offering, the market price of Princeville quickly rose above $5 per share. Rights that traded as low as 1 1/2 cents rose in price to nearly $2 only a few weeks later.

Investing in Risk Arbitrage

Risk arbitrage is a highly specialized area of value investing. Arbitrage, as noted earlier, is a riskless transaction that generates profits from temporary pricing inefficiencies between markets. Risk arbitrage, however, involves investing in far-from-riskless takeover transactions. Spinoffs, liquidations, and corporate restructurings, which are sometimes referred to as long-term arbitrage, also fall into this category.

Risk arbitrage differs from the purchase of typical securities in that gain or loss depends much more on the successful completion of a business transaction than on fundamental developments at the underlying company. The principal determinant of investors' return is the spread between the price paid by the investor and the amount to be received if the transaction is successfully completed. The downside risk if the transaction fails to be completed is usually that the security will return to its previous trading level, which is typically well below the takeover price.

The quick pace and high stakes of takeover investing have attracted many individual investors and speculators as well as professional risk arbitrageurs. It is my view that those arbitrageurs with the largest portfolios possess an advantage that smaller investors cannot easily overcome. Due to the size of their holdings, the largest arbitrageurs can afford to employ the best lawyers, consultants, and other advisors to acquire information with a breadth, depth, and timeliness unavailable to other investors. As we have learned from recent criminal indictments, some have even enjoyed access to inside information, although their informational edge was great even without circumventing the law.

The informational advantage of the largest risk arbitrageurs is not so compelling in situations such as long-term liquidations, spinoffs, and large friendly tender offers. In the largest friendly corporate takeovers, for example, the professional risk-arbitrage community depletes its purchasing power relatively quickly, leaving an unusually attractive spread for other investors. A careful and selective smaller investor may be able to profitably exploit such an opportunity.

At times of high investor uncertainty, risk-arbitrage-related securities may become unusually attractive. The December 1987 takeover of Becor Western Inc. by B-E Holdings, Inc., fit this description. In June 1987 Becor sold its aerospace business for $109.3 million cash. This left the company with $185 million in cash (over $11 per share) and only $30 million in debt. The company also operated an unprofitable but asset-rich mining-machinery business under the Bucyrus-Erie name.

The offer by B-E Holdings to buy Becor Western was the last in a series of offers by several suitors. The terms of this proposed merger called for Becor holders to receive either $17 per share in cash or a package of the following:

> $3 principal amount of 12.5 percent one-year senior notes in B-E Holdings;
>
> $10 principal amount of 12.5 percent fifteen-year senior debentures in B-E Holdings;
>
> 0.2 shares preferred stock in B-E Holdings, liquidation preference $25; and
>
> 0.6 warrants to buy common stock in B-E Holdings at $.01 per share.

A maximum of 57.5 percent of Becor shares were eligible to receive the cash consideration. Assuming that all stockholders elected to receive cash for as many shares as possible, each would receive per share of Becor owned:

> $9.775 cash
>
> $1.275 principal amount one-year notes
>
> $4.25 principal amount fifteen-year debentures
>
> .085 shares preferred stock
>
> .255 warrants

The cash option was almost certain to be worth more than the package of securities. Thus the total value of the consideration to holders who elected cash was greater than for those who did not. Nevertheless, a small proportion of Becor holders failed to choose the cash alternative, increasing the value to be received by the vast majority of holders who did.

What made Becor particularly attractive to investors was that in the aftermath of the 1987 stock market crash, the shares fell in price to below $10. Investors could thus purchase Becor stock for less than the underlying cash on the company's books, and for an amount approximately equal to the cash that would be distributed upon consummation of the merger, which was expected either in December 1987 or January 1988.

The shares were a real bargain at $10, whether or not the

merger occurred. The total value of the merger consideration was certainly greater than the $10 stock price—the cash component alone was nearly $10. Moreover, there was nearly enough cash on the books of B-E Holdings pro forma for the merger to retire the one-year notes. These appeared to be worth close to par value. Based on the market price of comparable securities, the fifteen-year debentures seemed likely to trade at a minimum of 50 percent of face value and perhaps significantly higher. The preferred stock was more difficult to evaluate, but 25 percent of its liquidation preference seemed conservative compared with other preferred issues. The warrants were virtually impossible to value. Even assuming they would trade at negligible prices, however, the total value of the merger consideration appeared to be at least $14 per share. .

Better still, the downside risk to investors was minimal. The book value of Becor was $12 per share, nearly all of it in cash. There were several sizable holders of Becor stock, a fact that increased the likelihood that underlying value would be realized in some fashion. Even if the merger were rejected by shareholders, a corporate liquidation appeared likely to yield similar value. At prices of $12 or below, investors faced little downside risk and the prospect of an appreciable and prompt return. As it turned out, the merger consideration was worth about $14.25 at market prices. Becor shares had declined in the wake of a broad market rout to a level below underlying value, creating an opportunity for value investors.

The Cycles of Investment Fashion:
The Risk-Arbitrage Cycle

Many participants in specialized areas of investing such as bankruptcy and risk arbitrage have experienced inferior results in recent years. One reason is the proliferation of investors in these areas. In a sense, there is a cycle of investment results attendant on any investment philosophy or market niche due to the relative popularity or lack of popularity of that approach at a particular time.

When an area of investment such as risk arbitrage or bankruptcy investing becomes popular, more money flows to specialists in the area. The increased buying bids up prices, increasing the short-term returns of investors and to some extent creating a self-fulfilling prophecy. This attracts still more investors, bidding prices up further. While the influx of funds helps to generate strong investment results for the earliest investors, the resultant higher prices serve to reduce future returns.

Ultimately the good investment performance, which was generated largely by those who participated in the area before it became popular, ends and a period of mediocre or poor results ensues. As poor performance continues, those who rushed into the area become disillusioned. Clients withdraw funds as quickly as they added them a few years earlier. The redemptions force investment managers to raise cash by reducing investment positions. This selling pressure causes prices to drop, exacerbating the poor investment performance. Eventually much of the "hot money" leaves the area, allowing the smaller number of remaining investors to exploit existing opportunities as well as the newly created bargains resulting from the forced selling. The stage is set for another up-cycle.

Risk arbitrage has undergone such a cycle during the past several years. In the early 1980s there were only a few dozen risk arbitrageurs, each of whom managed relatively small pools of capital. Their repeated successes received considerable publicity, and a number of new arbitrage boutiques were established. The increased competition did not immediately destroy the investment returns from risk arbitrage; the supply of such investments increased at the same time, due to a simultaneous acceleration in corporate takeover activity.

By the late 1980s many new participants had entered risk arbitrage. Relatively unsophisticated individual investors and corporations had become significant players. They tended to bid up prices, which resulted in narrower "spreads" between stock prices and deal values and consequently lower returns with more risk. Excess returns that previously had been available from arbitrage investing disappeared.

In 1990 several major takeovers fell through and merger activity slowed dramatically. Many risk arbitrageurs experienced significant losses, and substantial capital was withdrawn from the area. Arbitrage departments at several large Wall Street firms were eliminated, and numerous arbitrage boutiques went out of business. This development serves, of course, to enhance the likelihood of higher potential returns in the future for those who continue to play.

It is important to recognize that risk-arbitrage investing is not a sudden market fad like home-shopping companies or closed-end country funds. Over the long run this area remains attractive because it affords legitimate opportunities for investors to do well. Opportunity exists in part because the complexity of the required analysis limits the number of capable participants. Further, risk arbitrage investments, which offer returns that generally are unrelated to the performance of the overall market, are incompatible with the goals of relative-performance-oriented investors. Since the great majority of investors avoid risk-arbitrage investing, there is a significant likelihood that attractive returns will be attainable for the handful who are able and willing to persevere.

Investing in Spinoffs

Spinoffs often present attractive opportunities for value investors. A spinoff is a distribution of the shares of a subsidiary company to the shareholders of the parent company. A partial spinoff involves the distribution (or, according to the definition of some analysts, the initial public offering) of less than 100 percent of the subsidiary's stock.

Spinoffs permit parent companies to divest themselves of

businesses that no longer fit their strategic plans, are faring poorly, or adversely influence investor perceptions of the parent, thereby depressing share prices. When a company owns one or more businesses involved in costly litigation, having a poor reputation, experiencing volatile results, or requiring an extremely complex financial structure, its share price may also become depressed. The goal in spinning off such businesses is to create parts with a combined market value greater than the present whole.

Many parent-company shareholders receiving shares in a spinoff choose to sell quickly, often for the same reasons that the parent company divested itself of the subsidiary in the first place. Shareholders receiving the spinoff shares will find still other reasons to sell: they may know little or nothing about the business that was spun off and find it easier to sell than to learn; large institutional investors may deem the newly created entity too small to bother with; and index funds will sell *regardless of price* if the spinoff is not a member of their assigned index. For reasons such as these, not to mention the fact that spinoffs frequently go unnoticed by most investors, spinoff shares are likely to initially trade at depressed prices, making them of special interest to value investors. Moreover, unlike most other securities, when shares of a spinoff are being dumped on the market, it is not because the sellers know more than the buyers. In fact, it is fairly clear that they know a lot less.

Wall Street analysts do not usually follow spinoffs, many of which are small capitalization companies with low trading volumes that cannot generate sufficient commissions to justify analysts' involvement. Furthermore, since a spinoff is likely to be in a different line of business from its corporate parent, analysts who follow the parent will not necessarily follow the spinoff. Finally, most analysts usually have more work than they can handle and are not eager to take on additional analytical responsibilities.

Some spinoff companies may choose not to publicize the attractiveness of their own stocks because they prefer a temporarily undervalued market price. This is because management often receives stock options based on initial trading prices; until these options are, in fact, granted, there is an incentive to hold the share price down. Consequently a number of spinoff companies make little or no effort to have the share price reflect underlying value. The management of companies with depressed share prices would usually fear a hostile takeover at a low price, however "shark-repellent," anti-takeover provisions inserted into the corporate bylaws of many spinoffs, serve to protect management from corporate predators.

Another reason that spinoffs may be bargain priced is that there is typically a two- or three-month lag before information on them reaches computer databases. A spinoff could represent the best bargain in the world during its first days of trading, but no computer-dependent investors would know about it.

Shares of spinoffs typically do not fit within institutional constraints and consequently are quickly sold by institutional investors. Consider, for example, the spinoff of InterTAN, Inc., by Tandy Corporation in late 1986. InterTAN had a book value of about $15 per share, net-net working capital after all debt of roughly $11 per share, and highly profitable Canadian and Australian retailing operations. Large operating losses in Europe camouflaged this profitability and caused a small overall loss. It was clear to anyone who looked behind the aggregate losses to the separate geographic divisions that the Canadian and Australian operations alone were worth considerably more than the price of $11 per share at which InterTAN stock was trading.

An institutional investor managing $1 billion might hold twenty-five security positions worth approximately $40 million each. Such an investor might have owned one million Tandy shares trading at $40. He or she would have received a spinoff of 200,000 InterTAN shares having a market value of $2.2 million. A $2.2 million position is insignificant to this investor; either the stake in InterTAN will be increased to the average position size of $40 million, or it will be sold. Selling the shares is the path of least resistance, since the typical institutional investor probably knows little and cares even less about

InterTAN. Even if that investor wanted to, though, it is unlikely that he or she could accumulate $40 million worth of InterTAN stock, since that would amount to 45 percent of the company at prevailing market prices (and that almost certainly would violate a different constraint about ownership and control.) Needless to say, the great majority of Tandy's institutional shareholders simply dumped their InterTAN shares. InterTAN received no Wall Street publicity, and brokers had no particular incentive to drum up interest in the stock. As a result, waves of institutional selling created a temporary supply-and-demand imbalance, and numerous value investors were able to accumulate large InterTAN positions at attractive prices. By 1989 the company had turned its money-losing operations around, Wall Street analysts who had once ignored the stock had suddenly fallen in love with it, and investors no longer worried about what could go wrong, focusing instead on what might go right. The shares peaked that year at 62 ¾.

Opportunities can sometimes arise not in the spinoff but in the parent-company shares. As an example, at the end of 1988 Burlington Northern, Inc. (BNI), which owned a major railroad and a natural resources company, spun off its investment in Burlington Resources, Inc. (BR), to shareholders. A number of unusual market forces were at work at the time that created an investment opportunity in the ongoing parent company, BNI. What happened is this: many investors held BNI primarily because of its ownership of BR, which represented about two-thirds of the dollar value of the combined company. A number of these investors apparently sold BNI before the spinoff was completed and bought the newly formed BR, causing BNI to decline in price relative to BR. This created an opportunity for other investors to buy BNI stock pre-spinoff and sell BR stock short in order to lock in a cost of approximately $19 per share for the newly separated railroad business. Since the railroad was expected by analysts to earn $3.50 per share and pay a $1.20 annual dividend, establishing an investment in the railroad at $19 appeared to be an attractive opportunity compared with both absolute yardsticks of value and with the prices of shares in comparable companies. By 1990 the shares had approximately doubled from the 1988 level.

Conclusion

This chapter has identified a number of niches where value investors sometimes find attractive opportunities. It is by no means an exhaustive list and is not meant to be. Rather it shows how securities in a variety of market sectors can become inefficiently priced, creating potential bargains for those willing to hunt for them.

The next two chapters offer in-depth examples of two areas of opportunity for value investors. Chapter 11 examines the conversion of thrifts from mutual to stock ownership and shows how the arithmetic of this very unusual transaction creates frequent opportunities for value investors. Chapter 12 explores the opportunities for investors in financially distressed and bankrupt securities. These chapters both elaborate on the theme of this one: that attractive opportunities to purchase undervalued investments arise with some frequency in a number of areas and that these opportunities can be identified and exploited by value investors.

11

Investing in Thrift Conversions

Mutual thrift institutions were first formed in this country in the mid-nineteenth century and today number in the thousands. The mutual form of ownership gave depositors comfort that they would be fairly treated since, in theory, they owned the institutions. Since 1983 the conversion of hundreds of mutual thrift institutions to stock ownership has created numerous opportunities for value investors. Negative publicity coupled with the economics of thrift conversions served to unduly depress the share prices of many thrifts.

Before deregulation in the late 1970s the thrift industry was managed, according to the old joke, by the 3-6-3 principle: take in deposits at 3 percent, lend them out at 6 percent, and be on the golf course by 3 o'clock. A thrift executive's life was simple, fairly remunerative, and of high status in the community. Before deregulation forced their hands, few thrift executives were willing to face the uncertainties of a mutual-to-stock conversion.

By the 1980s, however, much of the thrift industry was hemorrhaging money. Financial deregulation had adversely impacted most thrifts in that the interest rates paid on deposit liabilities were suddenly allowed to fluctuate with market interest rates, while most thrift assets, in the form of home mortgage loans, bore fixed interest rates. For many thrifts, the cost of funds soon rose above the yield on their assets, resulting in a negative interest rate spread.

The Garn-St. Germain Act of 1982 permitted thrifts to engage in new, increasingly risky lending and investing activities, ultimately resulting in hundreds of billions of dollars in losses, which rendered numerous thrifts insolvent. Despite a proliferation in the early 1980s of accounting gimmickry designed to prop up the net worth of troubled institutions, many thrifts desperately needed additional capital to survive. Money-losing thrifts were generally unable to raise new funds, and those that were mutually owned remained mutually owned. Only profitable and adequately capitalized thrifts were in a position to sell shares by converting to stock ownership, and many of them attempted to do so.

In a typical initial public offering (IPO) all preoffering shares are owned by insiders, who typically bought in earlier at a small fraction of the offering price. To illustrate the diluting effect of a typical underwriting, if insiders have bought one million shares of XYZ at $1 per share and the public is subsequently offered one million newly issued shares at $11 each, there will then be two million shares outstanding with total proceeds to the company of $12 million (ignoring underwriting costs). The pro forma book value of the company's stock is $6 per share. The public's investment has been diluted by $5 per share (45 percent of the purchase price), while the insiders have gained a windfall of the same $5 per share.

Thrift conversions work differently. A thrift institution with a net worth of $10 million might issue one million shares of stock at $10 per share. Again ignoring costs of the offering, the proceeds of $10 million are added to the institution's preexisting net worth, resulting in pro forma shareholders' equity of $20 million. Since the one million shares sold on the IPO are the only shares outstanding, pro forma net worth is $20 per share. The preexisting net worth of the institution joins the investors' own funds, resulting immediately in a net worth per share greater than the investors' own contribution.

The mechanics of a mutual-to-stock conversion are fairly simple. Depositors in a converting thrift have a preemptive right to purchase shares. Management is typically granted the right to purchase shares alongside depositors. Remaining shares are offered to the general public, with preference sometimes given to customers or to anyone living in the thrift's geographic area.

So long as the thrift has positive business value before the conversion, the arithmetic of a thrift conversion is highly favorable to investors. Unlike any other type of initial public offering, in a thrift conversion there are no prior shareholders; all of the shares in the institution that will be outstanding after the offering are issued and sold on the conversion. The conversion proceeds are added to the preexisting capital of the institution, which is indirectly handed to the new shareholders without cost to them. In a real sense, investors in a thrift conversion are buying their own money and getting the preexisting capital in the thrift for free.

There is another unique aspect to thrift conversions. Unlike many IPOs, in which insiders who bought at very low prices sell some of their shares at the time of the offering, in a thrift conversion insiders virtually always buy shares alongside the public and at the same price. Thrift conversions are the only investment in which both the volume and price of insider buying is fully disclosed ahead of time and in which the public has the opportunity to join the insiders on equal terms.

The twin attractions of buying on equal terms with insiders and the favorable arithmetic of a thrift conversion make for a compelling investment opportunity as long as the preconversion thrift has a positive value. Many thrifts, of course, are worth less than their stated book value, and some are insolvent. Funds raised on the conversion of such institutions would pay to resolve preexisting problems rather than add to preexisting value.

Why were thrift stocks so depressed in the 1980s? The sell side of Wall Street has historically employed few thrift analysts, and the buy side even fewer. The handful of sell-side analysts on duty typically followed only the ten or twenty largest public thrifts, primarily those based in California and New York. No major Wall Street house was able to get a handle on all of the many hundreds of converted thrifts, and few institutional investors even made the effort. As a result, shares in new thrift conversions were frequently issued at an appreciable discount to the valuation multiples of other publicly traded thrifts in order to get investors to notice and buy them.

Of course, fundamental investment analysis applies to thrifts as it would to other businesses. Thrifts incurring high risks, such as expanding into exotic areas of lending or venturing far from home, should simply be avoided as unanalyzable. Thrifts speculating in newfangled instruments such as junk bonds or complex mortgage securities (those based on interest or principal only, for example) should be shunned for the same reason. A simple rule applies: if you don't quickly comprehend what a company is doing, then management probably doesn't either. This initial test limits investors to low-risk thrifts. This does not mean that investors could not profit from investing in risky institutions but rather that the potential return is not usually justified by the risk and uncertainty. Owing to the high degree of financial leverage involved in thrifts, there can be no margin of safety from investing in the shares of thinly capitalized financial institutions that own esoteric or risky assets.

While all businesses should be valued conservatively, conservatism is even more important in the case of highly leveraged financial institutions where operating risks are magnified by the capital structure. In evaluating such thrifts, book value is usually a low estimate of private-market value; most thrift takeovers occur at a premium to book value. Investors should adjust book value upward, however, to reflect understated assets, such as appreciated investment securities, below-market leases, real estate carried below current worth, and the value of a stable, low-cost deposit base. Similarly book value should be adjusted downward to reflect balance sheet intangibles, bad loans, and investments worth less than cost.

As part of the fundamental analysis of a thrift, its earnings should be adjusted for such nonrecurring items as securities gains and losses, real estate gains and losses, branch sales, real estate development profits, and accounting changes. Quality of earnings is extremely important since earnings derived from the recurring spread between interest earned on loans and interest paid on deposits are far more valuable than nonrecurring gains or volatile income from loan origination fees. Thrifts with low overhead costs are preferable to high-cost institutions both because they are more profitable and because they enjoy greater flexibility in times of narrow interest rate spreads.

Although thrift conversions are attractive, they are not a sure thing. While many of the thrift conversions of the 1980s ultimately proved rewarding to investors, there was never certainty about the outcome. There are many risks in any thrift investment, including asset quality, interest rate volatility, management discretion, and the unpredictable actions of competitors. Investors, as always, must analyze each potential thrift conversion investment not as an instance of an often attractive market niche but individually on its merits.

Jamaica Savings Bank

In June 1990 Jamaica Savings Bank converted from mutual to stock ownership through a newly formed holding company, JSB Financial (JSB). It is important to recall the macroeconomic context of this share offering. At the time of the JSB conversion, the United States had experienced a nationwide real estate downturn. Estimates of the total cost of the thrift industry bailout were reaching as high as $500 billion. Lending standards had been tightened for real estate borrowers in almost all regions. Most thrift and bank stocks had declined sharply in price, and many troubled institutions had been seized by federal regulators. Amidst these circumstances JSB made the improbable attempt to convert to public ownership.

JSB was not a typical thrift. Organized in 1866 in New York, it had on December 31, 1989, total assets of $1.5 billion and retained earnings of $197.1 million, a ratio of tangible capital to total assets of 13.5 percent prior to conversion. This was among the highest ratios in the country. Two-thirds of the assets of JSB were held in U.S. Treasury and other federal agencies' securities or cash equivalents, while only 30 percent was in loans, virtually all residential mortgages. JSB was in a class by itself: liquid, well capitalized, and without material business risk.

Depositors in JSB were offered the opportunity of buying 16 million shares at $10 each. The economics of a thrift conversion are such that even with JSB's obvious merits, the shares were offered to investors at only 47 percent of book value and a pro forma price/earnings multiple of ten times. The gloomy real estate environment and the depressed market for thrift stocks no doubt contributed to the low initial offering price.

As an investment JSB was extremely low risk in every respect. The credit risk was minimal, the high capital ratio reflected low financial leverage, and the stock sold well below JSB's tangible book value, a yardstick of its underlying worth.

One interesting way to evaluate the risk of investing in JSB was to consider that half the proceeds from the stock conversion, or $80 million, were to be retained at the holding company. This cash represented excess capital that could be used to repurchase JSB shares subsequent to the public offering. If the cash had been used in its entirety to repurchase JSB shares at two-thirds of book value (a 40 percent premium to the IPO price), the company could have repurchased one-third of the shares of JSB that had just been issued.

While most shareholders might have chosen not to sell at that price, the effect of such a program would almost certainly have been to raise the price of JSB shares. In fact, the pro forma book value per share, adjusted to reflect this hypothetical repurchase, would have increased from $21.12 to $25.00, an 18 percent increase. This illustrates the opportunity to investors of owning a thrift that is financially capable of and willing (as JSB indicated it was) to repurchase its shares cheaply.

Investors in JSB stood to profit in several ways. The earnings appeared likely to grow as the excess capital was deployed. Book value would also grow due to earnings retention. Management moreover was dedicated to enhancing shareholder value through an aggressive stock repurchase program; this would increase both earnings and book value per share. Indeed, management purchased a significant amount of stock in the IPO for itself. As it turned out, the first trade in JSB took place at a 30 percent premium to the offering price, and the shares remained at a premium even when the stock market slumped later in the year.

Conclusion

Thrift conversions, such as that of Jamaica Savings Bank, are an interesting part of the financial landscape. More significantly, they illustrate the way the herd mentality of investors can cause all companies in an out-of-favor industry, however disparate, to be tarred with the same brush.

The arithmetic of a thrift conversion is surely compelling. Yet except for brief interludes when investing in thrifts was popular among individual investors, this area has been virtually ignored. Only a small number of professional investors persisted in identifying this source of value-investment opportunities and understanding the reasons for its existence over a number of years.

12

Investing in Financially Distressed and Bankrupt Securities

As we have learned from the history of the junk-bond market, investors have traditionally attached a stigma to the securities of financially distressed companies, perceiving them as highly risky and therefore imprudent. Financially distressed and bankrupt securities are analytically complex and often illiquid. The reorganization process is both tedious and highly uncertain. Identifying attractive opportunities requires painstaking analysis; investors may evaluate dozens of situations to uncover a single worthwhile opportunity.

Although the number of variables is high in any type of investing, the issues that must be considered when investing in the securities of financially distressed or bankrupt companies are greater in number and in complexity. In addition to comparing price to value as one would for any investment, investors in financially distressed securities must consider, among other things, the effect of financial distress on business results; the

189

availability of cash to meet upcoming debt-service requirements; and likely restructuring alternatives, including a detailed understanding of the different classes of securities and financial claims outstanding and who owns them. Similarly, investors in bankrupt securities must develop a thorough understanding of the reorganization process in general as well as the specifics of each situation being analyzed.

Because most investors are unable to analyze these securities and unwilling to invest in them, the securities of financially distressed and bankrupt companies can provide attractive value-investment opportunities. Unlike newly issued junk bonds, these securities sell considerably below par value where the risk/reward ratio can be attractive for knowledgeable and patient investors.

Financially Distressed and Bankrupt Businesses

Companies get into financial trouble for at least one of three reasons: operating problems, legal problems, and/or financial problems. A serious business deterioration can cause continuing operating losses and ultimately financial distress. Unusually severe legal problems, such as those that plagued Johns Manville, Texaco, and A. H. Robins, caused tremendous financial uncertainty for these companies, leading them ultimately to seek bankruptcy court protection. Financial distress sometimes results almost entirely from the burdens of excessive debt; many of the junk-bond issuers of the 1980s shared this experience.

Financial distress is typically characterized by a shortfall of cash to meet operating needs and scheduled debt-service obligations. When a company runs short of cash, its near-term liabilities, such as commercial paper or bank debt, may not be refinanceable at maturity. Suppliers, fearing that they may not be paid, curtail or cease shipments or demand cash on delivery, exacerbating the debtor's woes. Customers dependent on an ongoing business relationship may stop buying. Employees may abandon ship for more secure or less stressful jobs.

Since the effect of financial distress on business results can vary from company to company, investors must exercise considerable caution in analyzing distressed securities. The operations of capital-intensive businesses are, over the long run, relatively immune from financial distress, while those that depend on public trust, like financial institutions, or on image, like retailers, may be damaged irreversibly. For some businesses the decline in operating results is limited to the period of financial distress. After a successful exchange offer, an injection of fresh capital, or a bankruptcy reorganization, these businesses recover to their historic levels of profitability. Others, however, remain shadows of their former selves.

The capital structure of a business also affects the degree to which operations are impacted by financial distress. For debtors with most or all of their obligations at a holding company one or more levels removed from the company's primary assets, the impact of financial distress can be minimal. Overleveraged holding companies, for example, can file for bankruptcy protection while their viable subsidiaries continue to operate unimpaired; Texaco entered bankruptcy while most of its subsidiaries did not file for court protection. Companies that incur debt at the operating-subsidiary level may face greater dislocations.

The popular media image of a bankrupt company is a rusting hulk of a factory viewed from beyond a padlocked gate. Although this is sometimes the unfortunate reality, far more often the bankrupt enterprise continues in business under court protection from its creditors. Indeed, while there may be a need to rebuild damaged relationships, a company that files for bankruptcy has usually reached rock bottom and in many cases soon begins to recover. As soon as new lenders can be assured of their senior creditor position, debtor-in-possession financing becomes available, providing cash to meet payroll, to restock depleted inventories, and to give confidence both to customers and suppliers. Since postpetition suppliers to the debtor have a senior claim to unsecured prepetition creditors, most suppliers renew shipments. As restocked inventories and increased confidence stimulate business and as deferred maintenance and delayed capital expenditures are undertaken, results may begin to improve. Cash usually starts to build (for a number of reasons to be discussed later). When necessary, new management can be attracted by the prospect of a stable and improving business situation and by the lure of low-priced stock or options in the reorganized company. While Chapter 11 is not a panacea, bankruptcy can provide a sheltered opportunity for some troubled businesses to return to financial health.

Issuer Responses to Financial Distress

There are three principal alternatives for an issuer of debt securities that encounters financial distress: continue to pay principal and interest when due, offer to exchange new securities for securities currently outstanding, or default and file for bankruptcy. A potential investor in distressed securities must consider each of these three possible scenarios before committing capital.

Financially troubled companies can try to survive outside bankruptcy by resorting to cost cutting, asset sales, or an infusion of outside capital. Such efforts can be successful, depending on the precise cause of the debtor's woes. Short-term palliatives, however, can contribute to the erosion of long-term business value. Efforts to conserve cash by cutting back inventory, stretching out accounts payable, or reducing salaries, for example, can get a business through a short-term crisis, but in the long run some of these measures may hurt relationships with customers, suppliers, and employees and result in a diminution of business value.

A second option for a company is to make an exchange offer to replace outstanding debt and, where relevant, preferred stock with new securities. The possibility of an exchange offer adds a strategic dimension to investing in financially distressed securities absent from most passive investments.

An exchange offer is an attempt by a financially distressed issuer to stave off bankruptcy by offering new, less-onerous securities in exchange for some or all of those outstanding. An exchange offer can serve as an out-of-court plan of reorganization. Sometimes an offer is made to exchange for only one security; perhaps the issuer needs only to extend an upcoming maturity. Other times most or all outstanding debt securities and, where relevant, preferred stock are offered the opportunity to exchange.

Exchange offers are difficult to complete. Typically they involve persuading debt holders (and preferred stockholders, if any) to accept less than one dollar's worth of new securities for each current dollar of claim against the debtor. The greatest difficulty in consummating an exchange offer is that, unlike stockholders, bondholders cannot be compelled to do anything. Depending on state law, a vote of 50 percent or 67 percent of the stockholders of a company is sufficient to approve a merger; the minority is compelled to go along. However, the majority of a class of bondholders cannot force the minority to accept an exchange offer. This results in a free-rider problem since the value of "holding out" is typically greater than the value of going along with a restructuring.

Suppose Company X needs to cut its debt from $100 million to $75 million and offers bondholders an opportunity to exchange their bonds, currently trading at fifty cents on the dollar, for new bonds of equal seniority valued at seventy-five. This offer may be acceptable to each holder; individually they would be willing to forego the full value of their claims in order to avoid the uncertainty and the delay of bankruptcy proceedings as well as the loss of the time-value of their money. They may be concerned, however, that if they agree to exchange while others do not, they will have sacrificed 25 percent of the value owed them when others have held out for full value. Moreover, if they make the sacrifice and others do not, the debtor may not be sufficiently benefitted and could fail anyway.

In that event those who exchanged would be rendered worse off than those who did not because, by holding a lower face amount of securities, they would have a smaller claim in bankruptcy.

An exchange offer is somewhat like the Prisoner's Dilemma. In this paradigm two prisoners, held incommunicado, are asked to confess to a crime. If neither confesses, they both go free. If both confess, they incur a severe punishment but not a lethal one. If one confesses and the other holds out, however, the holdout will be executed. If they could collude, both prisoners would hold out and go free; held in isolation, each fears that the other might confess.

The Prisoner's Dilemma is directly applicable to the bondholders in an exchange offer. Each might be willing to go along if he or she could be certain that other holders would also, but since no bondholder could be certain of others' cooperation, each has a financial incentive to hold out. Exchange offers often require a very high acceptance rate in order to mitigate this problem. If all bondholders could be brought together, there might be a chance to achieve voluntary cooperation. Historically, however, bondholders have been a disparate group, not always even identifiable by the debtor and hard to bring together for negotiations.

One way to overcome the free-rider problem is a technique known as a prepackaged bankruptcy, in which creditors agree to a plan of reorganization prior to the bankruptcy filing. Because negotiations have already been completed, a prepackaged bankruptcy is reasonably expected to be dispatched in months rather than years; the duration is not much greater than the time involved in completing an exchange offer. The advantage of a prepackaged bankruptcy over an exchange offer is that since a majority in number and two-thirds of the dollar amount of each creditor class must approve a bankruptcy plan, up to one-third of the dollar amount of a class can be compelled to go along with the other creditors, effectively eliminating the free-rider problem. It seems likely that there will be increased use of the prepackaged bankruptcy in future efforts to restructure overleveraged companies in order to expedite the reorganization process, avoid the high administrative costs of a traditional Chapter 11 filing, and circumvent the free-rider problem.

If measures to keep the patient alive prove unsuccessful, the third option is to file for court protection under Chapter 11 of the federal bankruptcy code and attempt to reorganize the debtor with a more viable capital structure. This is typically a last resort, however, for there is still considerable stigma attached to bankruptcy.

The Implications of a Bankruptcy Filing

Filing for bankruptcy halts efforts by creditors (lenders) to collect repayment from the debtor (borrower). Payment of principal and interest other than that due on fully secured debt is suspended. Payments to trade creditors and even employees are withheld. The different classes of creditors—secured, senior, and junior lenders, trade creditors, employees, and others—will be dealt with in a plan or sometimes competing plans of reorganization proposed and supported by either the debtor and/or by a major creditor group or groups. As stated previously, to be confirmed a plan must be approved by the bankruptcy judge as well as by a majority in number and two-thirds in dollar amount of each class of creditors.

The interests of a bankrupt debtor and its creditors can and frequently do diverge considerably. The debtor, seeking to emerge from bankruptcy as strong as possible, may attempt to maximize postreorganization cash and minimize postreorganization debt. Similarly the debtor may try to maintain high levels of capital spending during the Chapter 11 process in order to ensure a viable business after reorganization. By contrast, creditors will generally prefer to maximize cash distributions to themselves. They may oppose what they consider to be excessive capital expenditures by the debtor during the reorganization process, preferring a cash buildup that will subsequently be distributed to them. These conflicting interests will be resolved during the negotiation of a plan of reorganization and finally by the bankruptcy court.

A company may use a bankruptcy filing to void leases and executory contracts such as long-term supply arrangements. In the past even labor agreements have been terminated under bankruptcy. The 1978 bankruptcy of Food Fair Stores resulted in a number of voided store leases, the present value of which became claims against the debtor. The 1985 bankruptcy of Wheeling Pittsburgh Steel resulted in the rejection of existing iron ore- and coal-purchase contracts, which were subsequently renegotiated at lower prices; suppliers such as Cleveland-Cliffs and Hanna Mining became substantial claimants in bankruptcy. Although this could no longer be done today, in 1983 Continental Airlines used a bankruptcy filing to void its labor agreement, effectively replacing a unionized work force with nonunion labor.

Owing to a debtor's ability to reject contracts of nearly all types, a bankrupt company is frequently in a position to become a low-cost competitor in its industry upon reorganization. Unprofitable, high-cost facilities are closed or sold, above-market lease costs are reduced to market levels, and a company's overstated assets are typically written down on its books to fair-market value, thereby reducing future depreciation charges. The bankruptcy process can sometimes serve as a salutary catharsis, allowing troubled firms the opportunity to improve their business operations.

For several reasons bankrupt companies tend to build up substantial cash balances. Costs may be reduced either through contract rejections or through ordinary cost-cutting efforts, resulting in increased cash flow. More of a company's free cash flow is retained as interest payments on unsecured debt are suspended and common and preferred dividend payments are halted. Many bankrupt firms have substantial net operating loss (NOL) carry-forwards, resulting from prior tax losses or from write-offs incurred during bankruptcy; these NOLs offset taxes currently due, also augmenting cash. Capital spending, in particular spending on unrelated diversification and on new or risky activities, is curtailed. Unrelated, unprofitable, or otherwise ill-fitting businesses may be divested, again resulting in cash buildup. Since cash is not available for distribution until a plan of reorganization is approved and consummated, cash will grow from compound interest earned on existing cash balances and from interest on interest. All this has led to what one leading bankruptcy advisor has termed the money-market theory of bankruptcy: if enough cash builds up, it can simplify the process of devising a plan of reorganization that is acceptable to all parties because there are no differences of opinion concerning the value of cash and because more creditors can be paid in full.

The Investment Attractions of Bankruptcy

Investing in bankrupt securities differs from investing in companies operating normally. An obvious difference is that in a solvent company, an investor can be relatively certain of what belongs to whom. In a bankruptcy the treatment of valid claims is precisely what is to be decided in court: the disposition of the assets is to be determined by the owners of the liabilities who, along with the equity owners, will receive the assets either directly or more typically in the form of newly issued securities of the reorganized debtor.

As mentioned in chapter 10, one attractive feature of bankruptcy investing is that the reorganization process can serve as a catalyst for realizing underlying value. An undervalued stock may remain cheap forever and an attractive bond may have to be held until a distant maturity date to pay off, but a bankrupt company will typically reorganize within two or three years of filing under Chapter 11. Upon emergence from bankruptcy, the firm's creditors typically exchange their claims for some combination of cash, new debt securities, and equity in the reorganized debtor.

Emergence from Chapter 11 also serves as a liquefying event for claimholders. Owners of small, illiquid trade claims or large amounts of bank debt will experience a substantial enhancement in the liquidity of their holdings. Maximum liquidity would come from an all-cash distribution, but even debt or equity securities would likely provide holders more liquidity than claims against a bankrupt debtor.

An additional attraction of bankruptcy investing is that bankrupt debt securities, particularly senior securities, are not very sensitive to fluctuations in the stock or bond market. Bankrupt securities tend to behave somewhat like risk-arbitrage investments; they fluctuate in price more with the progress of the reorganization than with the overall market.

The Three Stages of Bankruptcy Investing

Michael Price of Mutual Series Fund, Inc., speaks of three stages of bankruptcy. The first stage, immediately after the Chapter 11 filing, is the time of greatest uncertainty but perhaps also of greatest opportunity for investors. The debtor's financial situation is in turmoil, financial statements may be late or unavailable, off-balance-sheet liabilities are not immediately evident, and the underlying business may not have stabilized. In addition the market for the debtor's securities is in disarray, with many holders forced to sell their holdings regardless of price.

The second stage of bankruptcy, involving the negotiation of a plan of reorganization, begins anywhere from a few months to several years after filing. By then analysts will have pored over the debtor's business and financial situation. Much more is known about the debtor, and security prices will incorporate the available information. Considerable uncertainty remains, however, about the eventual plan of reorganization. The treatment of various classes of creditors is still to be resolved.

The third and final stage of bankruptcy occurs between the finalization of a reorganization plan and the debtor's emergence from bankruptcy. Unless the plan is contested, is rejected by one or more classes of creditors, or falls through because a key condition is not met, this stage usually takes three months to one year. Although the time frame and legal process are less certain, the last stage most closely resembles a risk-arbitrage investment.

Each stage of bankruptcy affords different opportunities to the investor. The best bargains appear amidst the uncertainty and high risk of the first stage. The lowest but most predictable returns are available in the third stage, after the reorganization plan becomes publicly available.

Risks of Investing in Financially Distressed and Bankrupt Securities

Investing in financially distressed and bankrupt securities requires patience to wait for the right situation and the right security at the right price and discipline to adhere to value-investing criteria. When properly implemented, troubled-company investing may entail less risk than traditional investing, yet offer significantly higher returns. When badly done, the results of investing in distressed and bankrupt securities can be disastrous; junior securities, for example, can be completely wiped out. The market for distressed and bankrupt securities is illiquid, and traders can take advantage of unsophisticated investors. Quoted prices may bear little relationship to actual trading levels, and an uninformed buyer can significantly over-pay. In a market where most buyers are highly sophisticated, caution is the order of the day for the ordinary investor.

Many things can go wrong with bankruptcy investments. For one thing, the rate of return is highly dependent on timing. In bankruptcy unsecured but "fully covered" claims (claims that will receive one hundred cents on the dollar upon reorganiza-tion are known as fully covered) in essence become zero-coupon bonds; with par received at the end of the reorganization process, the rate of return to buyers depends on the duration of the bankruptcy. An investor who anticipates a long bankruptcy would naturally pay less than a more optimistic investor if he or she is to achieve the same rate of return.

The risk of investing in financially distressed and bankrupt securities varies with the specifics of each situation. At the riskiest end of the spectrum are highly competitive or fashion-oriented businesses dependent on a limited number of their key personnel and owning few tangible assets; companies that sell customized or user-specific products; and financial companies that are particularly dependent on investor and customer confidence. Examples include Ames Department Stores in the fiercely competitive discount store market and Integrated Resources, a highly leveraged financial-services company.

At the low-risk end of the spectrum are overleveraged capital-intensive debtors, possibly having monopoly or near-monopoly positions in their industries, and businesses producing homogeneous or undifferentiated products. Low-risk bankruptcies also do not have public-policy legal issues to be resolved. The secured bonds of Public Service Company of New Hampshire, an electric utility, or of Jones & Laughlin Steel, a subsidiary of LTV Corporation, a major integrated steel producer, are located at the low-risk end of the spectrum.

Investors should be wary of purchasing or holding the fixed-income securities of rapidly deteriorating businesses. It is easy to look at the apparent asset protection of a bond while ignoring earnings or cash flow problems. When a business loses cash from operations even before interest expense, it will often experience accelerating losses, especially if it is highly leveraged. If a turnaround does not come quickly, it may not come at all.

Although no investor can ignore price, investors in distressed or bankrupt securities must make price a primary focus. Both casual observers and some full-time academics tend to think of the financial markets as efficient and continuous, with prices determined by underlying business developments. By contrast, the market for a distressed or bankrupt bond may consist of only a few buyers and sellers and sometimes only the market-makers themselves. In an illiquid market the price at which a security transaction takes place is determined not so much by investment fundamentals as by the trading savvy of the participants. In the illiquid market for distressed and bankrupt bonds, being a smart trader may sometimes be more important than being a smart analyst.

The Financially Distressed and Bankrupt Security Investing Process

Investors in financially distressed and bankrupt securities must concentrate on the corporate balance sheet. Like knowing the opposing lineups at a baseball game, understanding the amounts and priorities of a company's liabilities can tell investors a great deal not only about how the various security holders are likely to be treated but also how the financial distress is likely to be resolved.

The first step is to value the assets of the debtor. Once the size of the pie is known, it is possible to consider how it may be divided. To facilitate this process, an investor must divide the debtor's assets into two parts: the assets of the ongoing business; and the assets available for distribution to creditors upon reorganization, such as excess cash, assets held for sale, and investment securities. Investors in AM International, Inc., senior claims received substantial amounts of AM's excess cash upon reorganization; investors in Braniff Airlines' first bankruptcy in 1983 received liquidating trust certificates backed by a direct interest in aircraft assets.

In valuing an ongoing business operating in Chapter 11, investors should employ each of the valuation methodologies described in chapter 8. In many instances the investor is in the difficult position of analyzing a moving target since the business of the debtor is unstable, if not in turmoil. It is essential that investors take into account any income statement and cash flow distortions caused by the Chapter 11 process itself. Interest earned on excess cash that builds up during bankruptcy, for example, will not be a source of income for the reorganized company. Similarly, interest expense on reinstated debt, which does not accrue during bankruptcy, will once again accrue. Then, again, the high investment banking, legal, and administrative costs of a Chapter 11 proceeding, often cumulatively totaling several percent or more of the value of the debtor's estate, will cease upon emergence from bankruptcy. Bankrupt companies may even intentionally "uglify" their financial statements (for example, by expensing rather than capitalizing certain expenses or by building excessive balance sheet reserves) in order to minimize the assets apparently available for distribution to creditors. This value is ultimately revealed after reorganization, but by then insiders have picked up cheap stock or options.

Analysis of the assets and liabilities of financially distressed or bankrupt companies must extend beyond the balance sheet however. Off-balance-sheet assets may include real estate carried below current value, an overfunded pension plan, patents owned, and the like. Off-balance-sheet liabilities may include underfunded pension plans, Internal Revenue Service, Environmental Protection Agency, Pension Benefit Guaranty Corporation (PBGC), and other governmental claims, and claims resulting from rejected executory contracts and leases. In recent steel industry bankruptcies, for example, Wheeling Pittsburgh Steel and LTV Corporation transferred their underfunded pension plans to the PBGC, resulting in a bankruptcy claim by the PBGC against Wheeling and protracted litigation between the PBGC and LTV.

Once a debtor's assets have been valued, investors should turn their attention to the liability side of the balance sheet. The liabilities of a bankrupt company are best evaluated in descending order of seniority. Secured debt should be evaluated first. If the value of the security interest is determined, whether through negotiation or a valuation proceeding, to be equal to or greater than the amount of claim, the claim is said to be fully secured or oversecured. An oversecured claim entitles the holder to postpetition accrued interest (interest that would have accrued during the bankruptcy proceeding) to the extent of the amount of oversecurity. If secured debt is determined to be less than fully secured, holders will typically receive value equal to the extent of their security plus a senior but unsecured claim against the debtor for the amount of the undersecurity.

There may be some investment opportunities in distressed securities at every rank in the debt hierarchy. Risk-averse investors will generally prefer to hold senior securities; the potential return from senior securities is frequently less than that available from junior claims, but the risk is also much lower. Senior securities are first in priority, and unless they are fully or almost fully repaid, junior classes are unlikely to receive significant value.

"Fulcrum securities"—the class of securities partly but not fully covered by asset value—can also be attractive investments at the right price, ranking midway on the risk spectrum. Fulcrum securities benefit most directly from value increases and likewise are most directly impaired by any value diminution.

Investing in junior securities can provide spectacular returns but can also prove disastrous. These securities often serve as out-of-the-money options—effectively, bets—on an improvement in operating results or an increase in value.

The common stock of bankrupt companies frequently trades considerably above its reorganization value, which is often close to zero. While there may be an occasional home run, as a rule investors should avoid the common stock of bankrupt entities at virtually any price; the risks are great and the returns very uncertain. Unsophisticated investors have lost a great deal of money buying the overpriced common stock of bankrupt companies, even after the unfavorable terms of the reorganization plan have been widely disseminated.

It is worth remembering that restructurings and bankruptcy reorganizations are negotiated processes. Negotiations can be affected by the relative bargaining strengths and weaknesses of the different classes of creditors, the skills of the negotiators, and the dollar amounts at stake.

By way of example, Ron Labow headed an investor group that bought up most of Wheeling Pittsburgh Steel's bank debt and dictated a reorganization plan that left him in control of the reorganized company. A blocking position—one-third of the outstanding amount of debt—in a small, closely held debt issue may enable that class to obtain better treatment than similar but more widely held debt issues. The holder of a blocking position in even the most junior bankrupt security, because of his or her ability to delay the debtor's emergence from bankruptcy, may gain far better treatment for his or her class than allowed by any allocation made strictly according to priority ranking. A blocking position is said to have "hold-up" value in two senses: the owner can hold up (delay) the bankruptcy process as well as hold up (rob) other classes of creditors, extracting nuisance value from what might otherwise be a nearly worthless claim.

HBJ Falls from Grace: An Opportunity in Financially Distressed Securities

The nature of opportunities that can exist in the market for distressed securities is well exemplified by the fall from grace of Harcourt Brace Jovanovich, Inc. (HBJ). HBJ was once a favorite of junk-bond investors and as recently as August 1989 had a total market capitalization of debt and equity securities of $4.6 billion. Its junk bonds traded above par value. At the time HBJ operated a well-known publishing business, an insurance company, and theme parks; the parks were up for sale. In September 1989 HBJ announced the sale of the theme parks to Anheuser-Busch for $1.1 billion ($1.0 billion net of taxes), a disappointing number to Wall Street analysts who had expected $1.5 billion. Bank debt was repaid with the after-tax proceeds. Logically the total capitalization should have declined from $4.6 billion to $3.6 billion. Instead, on January 31, 1990, the total market capitalization was only $1 billion, a decline of more than two-thirds from the implied capitalization only four months earlier. The magnitude of this decline can be explained only in the context of the shattering of investors' perceptions of Harcourt as "good junk." Once it became apparent that the company was seriously overleveraged, widespread selling took place, and security prices plunged.

Price decline alone does not make a security a bargain; an appreciable discount from underlying value is also required. In the case of HBJ the subordinated bonds were now an attractive bargain, for in January 1990 the business was almost certainly worth between $1.4 and $1.7 billion and possibly even more. (This valuation was borne out by the $1.5 billion takeover offer made by General Cinema Corporation a year later; the subordinated bonds were to receive nearly fifty cents on the dollar.) The face value of senior debt was only about $800 million, leaving between $600 million and $900 million of value against $950 million of subordinated debt. Trading at twenty-five cents on the dollar, this debt was extraordinarily attractive even under a pessimistic valuation scenario and even if business results worsened. In fact, in bankruptcy the value of these subordinated bonds would ultimately have been enhanced because interest payments to senior unsecured debt holders would be halted; any cash savings would accumulate mostly to the benefit of the subordinated bonds.[1]

Distressed Bonds Versus Optimistic Stock: Intermarket Arbitrage in Bank of New England Securities

Many times security prices in the stock market will be inconsistent with those in the bond market, as if investors in one market do not communicate with those in another. Financial distress created such an opportunity in the debt and equity securities of the Bank of New England Corporation (BNE). A large loss announced in January 1990 caused the subordinated bonds of BNE to plunge to 10 to 13 from levels in the 70s. At the same time the common stock of the Bank of New England traded at approximately $3.50 per share.

Overall BNE had roughly $700 million face amount of senior and subordinated debentures outstanding with a total market value of less than $100 million. The common stock, which was, of course, junior to the holding company bonds, had a total market capitalization of approximately $250 million.

Opportunistic investors bought the BNE bonds and sold BNE common stock short to lock in an apparent valuation disparity. Specifically, investors could purchase the bonds at 10 to 13 and sell short common stock in equal dollar amounts. A buyer of $1 million face amount of subordinated bonds at 10½ (for $105,000) could sell short 30,000 shares of common stock at $3.50 for equivalent net proceeds. Performing these simultaneous transactions appeared to be a low-risk strategy under any conceivable scenario.

If BNE became insolvent (as happened in early 1991), for example, bondholders would at worst lose their investment and might possibly achieve some recovery; the common stock would certainly be rendered worthless. The loss on the bonds would at least be offset by the gain on the short sale of common stock. In addition, investors would earn interest on the short-sale proceeds and might receive one or more interest payments from BNE (two semiannual coupons, as it turned out).

If BNE survived, the bonds seemed likely to rally by a greater percentage than the common stock. If the common stock tripled to $10.50 amidst a surprising recovery, for example, the bonds seemed likely to trade well above the 30 to 40 level that bondholders would need to break even. Again, investors would also benefit from interest payments received on the bonds as well as interest earned on the short credit balance.

Another possible scenario was a financial restructuring, whereby BNE would offer bondholders the opportunity to convert into equity. This alternative, which was seriously considered by the bank but ultimately proved to be unworkable, would have been highly favorable for those who were long bonds and short stock. The bonds would have benefitted from the premium above market that the company would have had to offer to induce holders to exchange, while the common stock would likely have declined due to the dilution and selling pressure resulting from the issuance of large amounts of common stock to bondholders.

Conclusion

Investing in bankrupt and financially distressed securities is a sophisticated, highly specialized activity. Each situation offers its own analytical challenges, risks, and opportunities. A relative handful of savvy, hard-nosed, and experienced practitioners compete for the available opportunities. Due to the stigma of bankruptcy, the uncertain outcomes of financial distress, and the analytical complexity involved, only a small number of investors will buy or even hold these securities. In fact, investment opportunities in this area result largely from the uneconomic behavior of other investors. When such an area becomes popular, as it did in early 1991, investors must make sure to avoid overpaying.

Perhaps Michael Milken was not crazy, merely greedy, when he extrapolated the investment opportunity in financially distressed and bankrupt securities to newly issued securities that he underwrote. It is certainly ironic that many of yesterday's junk-bond managers and analysts have become today's financially distressed and bankrupt players.

This chapter only touches on some of the reasons why financially distressed and bankrupt securities may be attractive to investors. It is certainly not a primer on how to successfully invest in these securities, and I do not expect readers to immediately become successful bankruptcy investors. My main point is that an extensive search for opportunities combined with insightful analysis can uncover attractive investment opportunities in all kinds of interesting places.

Notes

1. Investors must distinguish the individual securities of a company from the company as a whole. It is possible that the stock of HBJ could be overvalued even as the bonds are bargain priced. Also, one bond can be attractive even as another is overpriced.

13

Portfolio Management and Trading

No book on investing would be complete without a discussion of trading and portfolio management. Trading—the process of buying and selling securities—can have a significant impact on one's investment results. Good trading decisions can sometimes add to an investment's profitability and other times can mean the difference between executing a transaction and failing to do so. Portfolio management encompasses trading activity as well as the regular review of one's holdings. In addition, an investor's portfolio management responsibilities include maintaining appropriate diversification, making hedging decisions, and managing portfolio cash flow and liquidity.

All investors must come to terms with the relentless continuity of the investment process. Although specific investments have a beginning and an end, portfolio management goes on forever. Unlike many areas of endeavor, there is no near-annuity of profitable business, no backlog of upcoming investment returns. Heinz ketchup will have a reasonably predictable volume of sales year in and year out. In a sense, its profits of tomorrow were partially earned yesterday when its franchise was established. Investors in marketable securities will not have predictable annual results, however, even if they possess shares representing fractional ownership of the same company. Moreover, attractive returns earned by Heinz may not correlate with the returns achieved by investors in Heinz; the price paid for the stock, and not just business results, determines their return.

The Importance of Liquidity in Managing an Investment Portfolio

Since no investor is infallible and no investment is perfect, there is considerable merit in being able to change one's mind. If an investor purchases a liquid stock such as IBM because he thinks that a new product will be successful or because he expects the next quarter's results to be strong, he can change his mind by selling the stock at any time before the anticipated event, probably with minor financial consequences. An investor who buys a nontransferable limited partnership interest or stock in a non-public company, by contrast, is unable to change his mind at any price; he is effectively locked in. When investors do not demand compensation for bearing illiquidity, they almost always come to regret it.

Most of the time liquidity is not of great importance in managing a long-term-oriented investment portfolio. Few investors require a completely liquid portfolio that could be turned rapidly into cash. However, unexpected liquidity needs do occur. Because the opportunity cost of illiquidity is high, no investment portfolio should be completely illiquid either. Most portfolios should maintain a balance, opting for greater illiquidity when the market compensates investors well for bearing it.

A mitigating factor in the tradeoff between return and liquidity is duration. While you must always be well paid to sacrifice liquidity, the required compensation depends on how long you will be illiquid. Ten or twenty years of illiquidity is far riskier than one or two months; in effect, the short duration of an investment itself serves as a source of liquidity. Investors making venture-capital investments, for example, must be exceptionally well compensated to offset the high probability of loss, the large proportion of the investment that is at risk (losses are often complete wipeouts), and the illiquidity experienced for the duration of the investment. The cost of illiquidity is very high in such situations, rendering venture capitalists virtually unable to change their minds and making it difficult for them to cash in even when the businesses they invested in are successful.

Liquidity can be illusory. As Louis Lowenstein has stated, "In the stock market, there is liquidity for the individual but not for the whole community. The distributable profits of a company are the only rewards for the community."[1] In other words, while any one investor can achieve liquidity by selling to another investor, all investors taken together can only be made liquid by generally unpredictable external events such as takeover bids and corporate-share repurchases. Except for such extraordinary transactions, there must be a buyer for every seller of a security.

In times of general market stability the liquidity of a security or class of securities can appear high. In truth liquidity is closely correlated with investment fashion. During a market panic the liquidity that seemed miles wide in the course of an upswing may turn out only to have been inches deep. Some securities that traded in high volume when they were in favor may hardly trade at all when they go out of vogue.

When your portfolio is completely in cash, there is no risk of loss. There is also, however, no possibility of earning a high return. The tension between earning a high return, on the one hand, and avoiding risk, on the other, can run high. The appropriate balance between illiquidity and liquidity, between seeking return and limiting risk, is never easy to determine.

Investing is in some ways an endless process of managing liquidity. Typically an investor begins with liquidity, that is, with cash that he or she is looking to put to work. This initial liquidity is converted into less liquid investments in order to earn an incremental return. As investments come to fruition, liquidity is restored. Then the process begins anew.

This portfolio liquidity cycle serves two important purposes. First, as discussed in chapter 8, portfolio cash flow—the cash flowing into a portfolio—can reduce an investor's opportunity costs. Second, the periodic liquidation of parts of a portfolio has a cathartic effect. For the many investors who prefer to remain fully invested at all times, it is easy to become complacent, sinking or swimming with current holdings. "Dead wood" can accumulate and be neglected while losses build. By contrast, when the securities in a portfolio frequently turn into cash, the investor is constantly challenged to put that cash to work, seeking out the best values available.

Reducing Portfolio Risk

The challenge of successfully managing an investment portfolio goes beyond making a series of good individual investment decisions. Portfolio management requires paying attention to the portfolio as a whole, taking into account diversification, possible hedging strategies, and the management of portfolio cash flow. In effect, while individual investment decisions should take risk into account, portfolio management is a further means of risk reduction for investors.

Appropriate Diversification

Even relatively safe investments entail some probability, however small, of downside risk. The deleterious effects of such improbable events can best be mitigated through prudent diversification. The number of securities that should be owned to reduce portfolio risk to an acceptable level is not great; as few as ten to fifteen different holdings usually suffice.

Diversification for its own sake is not sensible. This is the index fund mentality: if you can't beat the market, be the market. Advocates of extreme diversification—which I think of as overdiversification—live in fear of company-specific risks; their view is that if no single position is large, losses from unanticipated events cannot be great. My view is that an investor is better off knowing a lot about a few investments than knowing only a little about each of a great many holdings. One's very best ideas are likely to generate higher returns for a given level of risk than one's hundredth or thousandth best idea.

Diversification is potentially a Trojan horse. Junk-bond-market experts have argued vociferously that a diversified portfolio of junk bonds carries little risk. Investors who believed them substituted diversity for analysis and, what's worse, for judgment. The fact is that a diverse portfolio of overpriced, subordinated securities, about each of which the investor knows relatively little, is highly risky. Diversification of junk-bond holdings among several industries did not protect investors from a broad economic downturn or credit contraction. Diversification, after all, is not how many different things you own, but how different the things you do own are in the risks they entail.

Hedging

Market risk—the risk that the overall stock market could decline—cannot be reduced through diversification but can be limited by hedging. An investor's choice among many possible hedging strategies depends on the nature of his or her underlying holdings. A diversified portfolio of large capitalization stocks, for example, could be effectively hedged through the sale of an appropriate quantity of Standard & Poor's 500 index futures. This strategy would effectively eliminate both profits and losses due to broad-based stock market fluctuations. If a portfolio were hedged through the sale of index futures, investment success would thereafter depend on the performance of one's holdings compared with the market as a whole.

A portfolio of interest-rate-sensitive stocks could be hedged by selling interest rate futures or purchasing or selling appropriate interest rate options. A gold-mining stock portfolio could be hedged against fluctuations in the price of gold by selling gold futures. A portfolio of import- or export-sensitive stocks could be partially hedged through appropriate transactions in the foreign exchange markets.

It is not always smart to hedge. When the available return is sufficient, for example, investors should be willing to incur risk and remain unhedged. Hedges can be expensive to buy and time-consuming to maintain, and overpaying for a hedge is as poor an idea as overpaying for an investment. When the cost is reasonable, however, a hedging strategy may allow investors to take advantage of an opportunity that otherwise would be excessively risky. In the best of all worlds, an investment that has valuable hedging properties may also be an attractive investment on its own merits.

By way of example, from mid-1988 to early 1990 the Japanese stock market rose repeatedly to record high levels. The market's valuation appeared excessive by U.S. valuation criteria, but in Japan the view that the stock market was indirectly controlled by the government and would not necessarily be constrained by underlying fundamentals was widely held. Japanese financial institutions, which had become accustomed to receiving large and growing annual inflows of funds for investment, were so confident that the market would continue to rise that they were willing to sell Japanese stock market puts (options to sell) at very low prices. To them sale of the puts generated immediate income; since in their view the market was almost certainly headed higher, the puts they sold would expire worthless. If the market should temporarily dip, they were confident that the shares being put back to them would easily be paid for out of the massive cash inflows they had come to expect.

Wall Street brokerage firms acted as intermediaries, originating these put options in Japan and selling them in private transactions to U.S. investors.[2] These inexpensive puts were in theory an attractive, if imprecise, hedge for any stock portfolio. Since the Japanese stock market was considerably overvalued compared with the U.S. market, investors in U.S. equities could hedge the risk of a decline in their domestic holdings through the purchase of Japanese stock market puts. These puts were much less expensive than puts on the U.S. market, while offering considerably more upside potential if the Japanese market declined to historic valuation levels.

As it turned out, by mid-1990 the Japanese stock market had plunged 40 percent in value from the levels it had reached only a few months earlier. Holders of Japanese stock market put options, depending on the specific terms of their contracts, earned many times their original investment. Ironically, these Japanese puts did not prove to be a necessary hedge; the Japanese stock market decline was not accompanied by a material drop in U.S. share prices. These puts were simply a good investment that might have served as a hedge under other circumstances.

The Importance of Trading

There is nothing inherent in a security or business that alone makes it an attractive investment. Investment opportunity is a function of price, which is established in the marketplace. Whereas some investors are company- or concept-driven, anxious to invest in a particular industry, technology, or fad without special concern for price, a value investor is purposefully driven by price. A value investor does not get up in the morning knowing his or her buy and sell orders for the day; these will be determined in the context of the prevailing prices and an ongoing assessment of underlying values.

Since transacting at the right price is critical, trading is central to value-investment success. This does not mean that trading in and of itself is important; trading for its own sake is at best a distraction and at worst a costly digression from an intelligent and disciplined investment program. Investors must recognize that while over the long run investing is generally a positive-sum activity, on a day-to-day basis most transactions have zero-sum consequences. If a buyer receives a bargain, it is because the seller sold for too low a price. If a buyer overpays for a security, the beneficiary is the seller, who received a price greater than underlying business value.

The best investment opportunities arise when other investors act unwisely thereby creating rewards for those who act intelligently. When others are willing to overpay for a security, they allow value investors to sell at premium prices or sell short at overvalued levels. When others panic and sell at prices far below underlying business value, they create buying opportunities for value investors. When their actions are dictated by arbitrary rules or constraints, they will overlook outstanding opportunities or perhaps inadvertently create some for others. Trading is the process of taking advantage of such mispricings.

Stay in Touch with the Market

Some investors buy and hold for the long term, stashing their securities in the proverbial vault for years. While such a strategy may have made sense at some time in the past, it seems misguided today. This is because the financial markets are prolific creators of investment opportunities. Investors who are out of touch with the markets will find it difficult to be in touch with buying and selling opportunities regularly created by the markets. Today with so many market participants having little or no fundamental knowledge of the businesses their investments represent, opportunities to buy and sell seem to present themselves at a rapid pace. Given the geopolitical and macroeconomic uncertainties we face in the early 1990s and are likely to continue to face in the future, why would abstaining from trading be better than periodically reviewing one's holdings?

Being in touch with the market does pose dangers, however. Investors can become obsessed, for example, with every market uptick and downtick and eventually succumb to short-term-oriented trading. There is a tendency to be swayed by recent market action, going with the herd rather than against it. Investors unable to resist such impulses should probably not stay in close touch with the market; they would be well advised to turn their investable assets over to a financial professional.

Another hazard of proximity to the market is exposure to stockbrokers. Brokers can be a source of market information, trading ideas, and even useful investment research. Many, however, are in business primarily for the next trade. Investors may choose to listen to the advice of brokers but should certainly confirm everything that they say. Never base a portfolio decision solely on a broker's advice, and always feel free to say no.

Buying: Leave Room to Average Down

The single most crucial factor in trading is developing the appropriate reaction to price fluctuations. Investors must learn to resist fear, the tendency to panic when prices are falling, and greed, the tendency to become overly enthusiastic when prices are rising. One half of trading involves learning how to buy. In my view, investors should usually refrain from purchasing a "full position" (the maximum dollar commitment they intend to make) in a given security all at once. Those who fail to heed this advice may be compelled to watch a subsequent price decline helplessly, with no buying power in reserve. Buying a partial position leaves reserves that permit investors to "average down," lowering their average cost per share, if prices decline.

Evaluating your own willingness to average down can help you distinguish prospective investments from speculations. If the security you are considering is truly a good investment, not a speculation, you would certainly want to own more at lower prices. If, prior to purchase, you realize that you are unwilling to average down, then you probably should not make the purchase in the first place. Potential investments in companies that are poorly managed, highly leveraged, in unattractive businesses, or beyond understanding may be identified and rejected.

Selling: The Hardest Decision of All

Many investors are able to spot a bargain but have a harder time knowing when to sell. One reason is the difficulty of knowing precisely what an investment is worth. An investor buys with a range of value in mind at a price that provides a considerable margin of safety. As the market price appreciates, however, that safety margin decreases; the potential return diminishes and the downside risk increases. Not knowing the exact value of the investment, it is understandable that an investor cannot be as confident in the sell decision as he or she was in the purchase decision.

To deal with the difficulty of knowing when to sell, some investors create rules for selling based on specific price-to-book value or price-to-earnings multiples. Others have rules based on percentage gain thresholds; once they have made X percent, they sell. Still others set sale price targets at the time of purchase, as if nothing that took place in the interim could influence the decision to sell. None of these rules makes good sense. Indeed, there is only one valid rule for selling: all investments are for sale at the right price.

Decisions to sell, like decisions to buy, must be based upon underlying business value.[3] Exactly when to sell—or buy— depends on the alternative opportunities that are available. Should you hold for partial or complete value realization, for example? It would be foolish to hold out for an extra fraction of a point of gain in a stock selling just below underlying value when the market offers many bargains. By contrast, you would not want to sell a stock at a gain (and pay taxes on it) if it were still significantly undervalued and if there were no better bargains available.

Some investors place stop-loss orders to sell securities at specific prices, usually marginally below their cost. If prices rise, the orders are not executed. If the prices decline a bit, presumably on the way to a steeper fall, the stop-loss orders are executed. Although this strategy may seem an effective way to limit downside risk, it is, in fact, crazy. Instead of taking advantage of market dips to increase one's holdings, a user of this technique acts as if the market knows the merits of a particular investment better than he or she does.

Liquidity considerations are also important in the decision to sell. For many securities the depth of the market as well as the quoted price is an important consideration. You cannot sell, after all, in the absence of a willing buyer; the likely presence of a buyer must therefore be a factor in the decision to sell. As the president of a small firm specializing in trading illiquid over-the-counter (pink-sheet) stocks once told me: "You have to feed the birdies when they are hungry."

If selling still seems difficult for investors who follow a value-investment philosophy, I offer the following rhetorical questions: If you haven't bought based upon underlying value, how do you decide when to sell? If you are speculating in securities trading above underlying value, when do you take a profit or cut your losses? Do you have any guide other than "how they are acting," which is really no guide at all?

Use a Broker to Whom You Are Important

Whether buying or selling, there are distinct advantages to finding and doing business with long-term-oriented stockbrokers who recognize that it is in their interest to build and maintain mutually beneficial relationships with clients. If customers feel that their best interests are being served and that brokerage commissions are a secondary consideration, long-term relationships are likely to ensue. By contrast, brokers who charge exorbitant commissions or routinely recommend trades designed more to generate commissions than investment profits will eventually lose customers. The challenge is to find one or more brokers with whom you feel comfortable.

An appropriate broker will possess a balance of experience and desire, a commitment to the investment business, and a willingness to sacrifice immediate commissions for the sake of long-term relationships. You want a broker with sufficient clout within his or her firm to provide you with access to analysts and traders, one with experience to handle your account properly and to know when to call you and when not to waste your time.

You don't want a totally inexperienced broker who is learning at your expense, a complacent broker satisfied with mediocre results, or one so successful that your account is relatively unimportant. Michael Price and Bill Ruane would have no problem capturing the undivided attention of any broker; they would be very important clients for anyone. Other investors must work harder to find one or more brokers to whom they will be important clients. One possibility is to develop a relationship with a fairly young but capable broker to whom your account is currently very important and one who will gain importance and clout within the firm over time.

Conclusion

This chapter has identified a number of issues that investors should consider in managing their portfolios. While individual personalities and goals can influence one's trading and portfolio management techniques to some degree, sound buying and selling strategies, appropriate diversification, and prudent hedging are of importance to all investors. Of course, good portfolio management and trading are of no use when pursuing an inappropriate investment philosophy; they are of maximum value when employed in conjunction with a value-investment approach.

Notes

1. Louis Lowenstein, *What's Wrong with Wall Street* (Reading, Mass.: Addison-Wesley, 1988), p. 43.

2. At times Wall Street also acted as principal in the sale of Japanese stock market put options, relying on option-pricing models to establish correct values for the puts they wrote and on "dynamic hedging strategies" to protect them from loss. Dynamic hedging operates very much like portfolio insurance, requiring the sale of increasing quantities of futures contracts as market prices decline.

3. Tax considerations may be an additional factor in the decision to sell.

14

Investment Alternatives for the Individual Investor

If this book were a fairy tale, perhaps it would have a happier ending. The unfortunate fact is that the individual investor has few, if any, attractive investment alternatives. Investing, it should be clear by now, is a full-time job. Given the vast amount of information available for review and analysis and the complexity of the investment task, a part-time or sporadic effort by an individual investor has little chance of achieving long-term success. It is not necessary, or even desirable, to be a professional investor, but a significant, ongoing commitment of time is a prerequisite. Individuals who cannot devote substantial time to their own investment activities have three alternatives: mutual funds, discretionary stockbrokers, or money managers.

Mutual Funds

Mutual funds are, in theory, an attractive alternative for the individual investor, combining professional management, low transaction costs, immediate liquidity, and reasonable diversification. In practice, they mostly do a mediocre job of managing money. There are, however, a few exceptions to this rule.

For one thing, investors should certainly prefer no-load over load funds; the latter charge a sizable up-front fee, which is used to pay commissions to salespeople. Unlike closed-end funds, which have a fixed number of shares that fluctuate in price according to supply and demand, open-end funds issue new shares and redeem shares in response to investor interest. The share price of open-end funds is always equal to net asset value, which is based on the current market prices of the underlying holdings. Because of the redemption feature that ensures both liquidity and the ability to realize current net asset value, open-end funds are generally more attractive for investors than closed-end funds.[1]

Unfortunately for their shareholders, because open-end mutual funds attract and lose assets in accordance with recent results, many fund managers are participants in the short-term relative-performance derby. Like other institutional investors, mutual fund organizations profit from management fees charged as a percentage of the assets under management; their fees are not based directly on results. Consequently, the fear of asset outflows resulting from poor relative performance generates considerable pressure to go along with the investment crowd.

Another problem is that open-end mutual funds have in recent years attracted (and even encouraged) "hot" money from speculators looking to earn quick profits without the risk or bother of direct stock ownership. Many highly specialized mutual funds (e.g., biotechnology, environmental, Third World) have been established in order to exploit investors' interests in the latest market fad. Mutual-fund-marketing organizations have gone out of their way to encourage and even incite investor enthusiasm, setting up retail mutual fund stores, providing hourly fund pricing, and authorizing switching among their funds by telephone. They do not discourage the mutual fund newsletters and switching services that have sprouted up to accommodate the "needs" of hot-money investors.

Some open-end mutual funds do have a long-term value-investment orientation. These funds have a large base of loyal, long-term-oriented shareholders, which reduces the risk of substantial redemptions that could precipitate the forced liquidation of undervalued positions into a depressed market. The Mutual Series Funds and the Sequoia Fund, Inc., are my personal favorites; the Sequoia Fund, Inc., has been completely closed to new investors in recent years, while some of the Mutual Series Funds periodically open to accommodate new investors.

Evaluating Discretionary Stockbrokers and Money Managers

Some stockbrokers function as money managers, having discretionary investment authority over some or all of their clients' funds. Practices such as these may entail serious conflicts of interest since compensation is made on the basis of trading commissions rather than investment results. Nevertheless, you would select a discretionary stockbroker just as you would choose a money manager. The questions to be asked are virtually identical. In both cases, while there are large pools of people from whom to choose, selecting someone to handle your money with prudence and fiduciary responsibility is never easy.

The ultimate challenge in selecting a stockbroker or money manager is understanding precisely what they do, evaluating the validity of their investment approaches (do they make sense?) and their integrity (do they do what is promised, and is it in your best interest?).

How do you begin to evaluate stockbrokers and money managers? There are several important areas of inquiry, and one or more personal interviews are absolutely essential. There is no better place to begin one's investigation than with personal ethics. Do they "eat home cooking"—managing their own money in parallel with their clients'? I can think of no more important test of the integrity of a manager and the likelihood of investment success than his or her own confidence in the approach pursued on behalf of clients. It is interesting to note that few, if any, junk-bond managers invested their own money in junk bonds. In other words, they ate out.

Another area of inquiry concerns the fair treatment of clients. Are all clients treated equally? If not, why not, and in what ways? Are transactions performed for all clients contemporaneously? If not, what method is used to ensure fairness?

A third area of interest concerns the likelihood of achieving good investment results. Specifically, does the broker or money manager oversee a reasonably sized portfolio, or have the assets under management grown exceedingly large? One way to judge is to examine the manager's track record since the assets under his or her control reached approximately the current level. Investors can also examine the records of other managers to determine in general how increased size affects performance. In my experience, large increases in assets under management adversely affect returns. The precise amount that can be managed successfully depends on the specific investment strategy employed as well as the skills of the manager under consideration.

A fourth area of inquiry concerns the investment philosophy of the manager. Does the broker or money manager have an intelligent strategy that is likely to result in long-term investment success? (Obviously in my view, a value-investment strategy would be optimal.) Does he or she worry about absolute returns, about what can go wrong, or is he or she caught up in the relative-performance game? Are arbitrary constraints and silly rules, such as remaining fully invested at all times, absent?

Evaluating Investment Results

The decision to employ an investment professional should only be made after a thorough analysis of the past investment performance of the individual or organization under consideration. Some questions are obvious: How long a track record is there? Was it achieved over one or more market and economic cycles? Was it achieved by the same person who will manage your money, and does it represent the complete results of this manager's entire investment career or only the results achieved during some favorable period? (Everyone, of course, will be able to extract some period of good performance even from a lengthy record of mediocrity.) Did this manager invest conservatively in down markets, or did clients lose money? Were the results fairly steady over time, or were they volatile? Was the record the result of one or two spectacular successes or of numerous moderate winners? If this manager's record turns mediocre after one or two spectacular successes are excluded, is there a sound reason to expect more home runs in the future? Is this manager still following the same strategy that was employed to achievehis or her past successes?

Obviously a manager who has achieved dismal long-term results is not someone to hire to manage your money. Nevertheless, you would not necessarily hire the best-performing manager for a recent period either. Returns must always be examined in the context of risk. Consider asking whether the manager was fully invested at all times or even more than 100 percent invested through the use of borrowed money. (Leverage is neither necessary nor appropriate for most investors.)

Contrariwise, if the manager achieved good results despite having held substantial amounts of cash and cash equivalents, this could indicate a low-risk approach. Were the investments in the underlying portfolio themselves particularly risky, such as the shares of highly leveraged companies? Conversely, did the manager reduce portfolio risk through diversification or hedging or by investing in senior securities?

When you get right down to it, it is simple to compare managers by their investment returns. As discussed in chapter 7, it is far more difficult—impossible except in retrospect—to evaluate the risks that managers incurred to achieve their results.

Investment returns for a brief period are, of course, affected by luck. The laws of probability tell us that almost anyone can achieve phenomenal success over any given measurement period. It is the task of those evaluating a money manager to ascertain how much of their past success is due to luck and how much to skill.

Many investors mistakenly choose their money managers the same way they pick horses at the race track. They see who has performed well lately and bet on them. It is helpful to recognize that there are cycles of investment fashion; different investment approaches go into and out of favor, coincident with recent fluctuations in the results obtained by practitioners. If a manager with a good long-term record has a poor recent one, he or she may be specializing in an area that is temporarily out of favor. If so, the returns achieved could regress to their long-term mean as the cycle turns over time; several poor years could certainly be followed by several strong ones.

Finally, one of the most important matters for an investor to consider is personal compatibility with a manager. If personal rapport with a financial professional is lacking, the relationship will not last. Similarly, if there is not a level of comfort with the particular investment approach, the choice of manager is a poor one. A conservative investor may not feel comfortable with a professional short-seller no matter how favorable the results; by contrast, an aggressive investor may not be compatible with a manager who buys securities and holds them.

Once a money manager has been hired, clients must monitor his or her behavior and results on an ongoing basis. The issues that were addressed in hiring a manager are the same ones to consider after you have hired one.

Conclusion

Once you choose to venture beyond U.S. Treasury bills, whatever you do with your money carries some risk. Don't think you can avoid making a choice; inertia is also a decision. It took a long time to accumulate whatever wealth you have; your financial well-being is definitely not something to trifle with. For this reason, I recommend that you adopt a value-investment philosophy and either find an investment professional with a record of value-investment success or commit the requisite time and attention to investing on your own.

Notes

1. Closed-end funds should never be purchased on the initial public offering (as discussed in chapter 3). However, there may be an opportunity to invest in closed-end mutual funds at an appreciable discount to net asset value after they have been issued and traded for a while. If the fund manager is capable and the fee structure is fair, a closed-end fund selling at least 10 percent below underlying net asset value may be attractive.

Glossary

Absolute-performance orientation—the tendency to evaluate investment results by measuring one's investment performance against an absolute standard such as the risk-free rate of return

Annuity—a stream of cash in perpetuity

Arbitrage—the practice of investing in risk-free transactions to take advantage of pricing discrepancies between markets (see **risk arbitrage**)

Arbitrageur—investor in risk-arbitrage transactions

Asked price (offer)—the price at which a security is offered for sale (see **bid price**)

Asset—something owned by a business or individual

Average down—to buy more of a security for less than one's earlier purchase price(s), resulting in a reduction of the average cost

Balance sheet—accounting statement of a company's assets, liabilities, and net worth

Bankruptcy—a legal state wherein a debtor (borrower) is temporarily protected from creditors (lenders); under Chapter 11 of the federal bankruptcy code, companies may continue to operate (see **Chapter 11**)

Bear market—an environment characterized by generally declining share prices (see **bull market**)

Beta—a statistical measure used by some academics and market professionals to quantify investment risk by comparing a security's or portfolio's historical price performance with that of the market as a whole

Bid price—the price a potential buyer is willing to pay for a security (see **asked price**)

Blocking position—the ownership of a sufficient percentage of a class of securities to prevent undesirable actions from occurring (a creditor owning one-third or more of a class of bankrupt debt securities is able to "block" approval of a plan of reorganization not to his or her liking)

Bond—a security representing a loan to a business or government entity

Book value—the historical accounting of shareholders' equity; this is, in effect, the residual after liabilities are subtracted from assets

Bottom-up investing—strategy involving the identification of specific undervalued investment opportunities one at a time through fundamental analysis

Breakup value—the expected proceeds if the assets of a company were sold to the highest bidder, whether as a going concern or not (see **liquidation value**)

Bull market—an environment characterized by generally rising share prices (see **bear market**)

Callable bond—a bond that may be retired by the issuer at a specified price prior to its contractual maturity (see **puttable bond**)

Call option—a contract enabling the owner to purchase a security at a fixed price on a particular date (see **put option**)

Cash flow—the cash gain or loss experienced by a business during a particular period of operations

Cash-pay securities—securities required to make interest or dividend payments in cash (see **non-cash-pay securities**)

Catalyst—an internally or externally instigated corporate event that results in security holders realizing some or all of a company's underlying value

Chapter 11—a section of the federal bankruptcy code whereby a debtor is reorganized as a going concern rather than liquidated (see **bankruptcy**)

Closed-end mutual fund—mutual fund having a fixed number of outstanding shares that trade based on supply and demand at prices not necessarily equal to underlying net asset value (see **open-end mutual fund**)

Collateralized bond obligation (CBO)—diversified investment pools of junk bonds that issue their own securities, usually in several tranches, each of which has risk and return characteristics that differ from those of the underlying junk bonds themselves

Commercial paper—short-term loans from institutional investors to businesses

Commission—a charge for transacting in securities

Complex securities—securities with unusual cash flow characteristics

Contingent-value rights—tradable rights that are redeemable for cash if a stock fails to reach specified price levels

Convertible arbitrage—arbitrage transactions designed to take advantage of price discrepancies between convertible securities and the securities into which they are convertible

Convertible bonds—bonds that can be exchanged for common stock or other assets of a company at a specified price

Coupon—the specified interest payment on a bond expressed as a percentage

Covered-call writing—the practice of purchasing common stocks and then selling call options against them

Cram-down security—security distributed in a merger transaction, not sold by an underwriter

Credit cycle—the ebb and flow in the availability of credit

Debtor-in-possession financing—loan to a bankrupt company operating in Chapter 11

Debt-to-equity ratio—the ratio of a company's outstanding debt to the book value of its equity; a measure of a company's financial leverage

Default—the status of a company that fails to make an interest or principal payment on a debt security on the required date

Default rate of junk bonds—calculated by many junk-bond-market participants as the dollar volume of junk-bond defaults occurring in a particular year divided by the total volume of junk bonds outstanding

Depreciation—an accounting procedure by which long-lived assets are capitalized and then expensed over time

Discount rate—the rate of interest that would make an investor indifferent between present and future dollars

Diversification—ownership of many rather than a small number of securities; the goal of diversification is to limit the risk of company-specific events on one's portfolio as a whole

Dividend—cash distributed by a company to its shareholders out of after-tax earnings

Earnings before interest, taxes, depreciation, and amortization (EBITDA)—a nonsensical number thought by some investors to represent the cash flow of a business

Earnings per share—a company's after-tax earnings divided by the total number of shares outstanding

Efficient-market hypothesis—speculative notion that all information about securities is disseminated and becomes fully reflected in security prices instantaneously

Employee Retirement Income Security Act of 1974 (ERISA)—legislation that requires institutional investors to act as fiduciaries for future retirees by adopting the "prudent-man standard" (see **prudent-man standard**)

Equity "stubs"—low-priced, highly leveraged stocks, often resulting from a corporate recapitalization (see **recapitalization**)

Exchange offer—an offer made by a company to its security holders to exchange new, less-onerous securities for those outstanding

"Fallen angels"—bonds of companies that have deteriorated beneath investment grade in credit quality

Financial distress—the condition of a business experiencing a shortfall of cash to meet operating needs and scheduled debt-service requirements

Friendly takeover—corporate acquisition in which the buyer and seller both support the transaction enthusiastically

Fulcrum securities—the class of securities whose strict priority bankruptcy claim is most immediately affected by changes in the debtor's value

Full position—ownership of as much of a given security as an investor is willing to hold

Fundamental analysis—analyzing securities based on the operating performance (fundamentals) of the underlying business

Ginnie Mae (GNMA)—pool of mortgages insured by the Government National Mortgage Association, a U.S. government agency

Going long—buying a security (see **short-selling**)

Goodwill amortization—the gradual expensing of the intangible asset known as goodwill, which comes into existence when a company is purchased for more than its tangible book value

Guaranteed-investment contract (GIC)—an insurance-company-sponsored investment product that automatically reinvests interest at a contractual rate

Hedge—an investment that, by appreciating (depreciating) inversely to another, has the effect of cushioning price changes in the latter

Holding company—a corporate structure in which one company (the holding company) is the owner of another

Hold-up value—benefits accruing to participants in a class of securities who are able to extract considerable nuisance value from the holders of other classes of securities

Illiquid security—a security that trades infrequently, usually with a large spread between the bid and asked prices (see **liquid security**)

Income statement—accounting statement calculating a company's profit or loss

Indexing—the practice of buying all the components of a market index, such as the Standard and Poor's 500 index, in proportion to the weightings of that index and then passively holding them

Initial public offering (IPO)—underwriting of a stock being offered to the public for the first time

Inside information—information unavailable to the public, upon which it is illegal to base transactions

Institutional investors—money managers, pension fund managers, and managers of mutual funds

Intangible asset—an asset without physical presence; examples include intellectual property rights (patents) or going-concern value (goodwill)

Interest—payment for the use of borrowed money

Interest-coverage ratio—the ratio of pretax earnings to interest expense

Interest-only mortgage security (IO)—interest payments stripped from a pool of mortgages which, for a given change in interest rates, fluctuates in value inversely to conventional mortgages (see **principal-only mortgage security**)

Interest rate reset—a promise made by an issuer to adjust the coupon on a bond at a specified future date in order to cause it to trade at a predetermined price

Internal rate of return (IRR)—calculation of the rate of return of an investment that assumes reinvestment of cash flows at the same rate of return the investment itself offers

Investment—an asset purchased to provide a return; investments, in contrast to speculations, eventually generate cash flow for the benefit of the owners (see **speculation**)

Investment banking—profession involving raising capital for companies as well as underwriting and trading securities, arranging for the purchase and sale of entire companies, providing financial advice, and opining on the fairness of specific transactions

Investment grade—fixed income security rated BBB or higher

Junk bond—fixed-income security rated below investment grade

Leveraged buyout (LBO)—acquisition of a business by an investor group relying heavily on debt financing

Liability—a debt or other obligation to pay

Liquidating distribution—cash or securities distributed to shareholders by a company in the process of liquidation

Liquidating trust—an entity established to complete a corporate liquidation

Liquidation value—the expected proceeds if the assets of a company were sold off, but not as part of an ongoing enterprise

Liquidity—having ample cash on hand

Liquid security—a security that trades frequently and within a narrow spread between the bid and asked prices

Making a market—acting as a securities dealer by simultaneously bidding for and offering a security

Margin of safety—investing at considerable discounts from underlying value, an individual provides himself or herself room for imprecision, bad luck, or analytical error (i.e., a "margin of safety") while avoiding sizable losses

Market price—the price of the most recent transaction in a company's publicly traded stock or bonds

Maturity—the date on which the face value of a debt security is due and payable

Merchant banking—an activity whereby Wall Street firms commit their own capital while acting as principal in investment-banking transactions

Merger—a combination of two corporations into one

Mutual fund—a pooled investment portfolio managed by professional investors

Net asset value (NAV)—the per share value of a mutual fund calculated by dividing the total market value of assets by the number of shares outstanding

Net-net working capital—net working capital less all long-term liabilities

Net operating-loss carryforward (NOL)—the carryforward of past losses for tax purposes, enabling a company to shield future income from taxation

Net present value (NPV)—calculation of the value of an investment by discounting future estimates of cash flow back to the present

Non-cash-pay securities—securities permitted to pay interest or dividends in kind or at a later date rather than in cash as due (see **cash-pay securities, pay-in-kind,** and **zero-coupon bond**)

Nonrecourse—the lender looks only to the borrowing entity for payment

Open-end mutual fund—mutual fund offering to issue or redeem shares at a price equal to underlying net asset value

Opportunity cost—the loss represented by forgone opportunities

Option—the right to buy (call) or sell (put) specified items at specified prices by specified dates

Over-the-counter (OTC)—the market for stocks not listed on a securities exchange (e.g., New York, American, Philadelphia, Boston, Pacific, Toronto)

Par—the face amount of a bond; the contractual amount of the bondholder's claim

Pay-in-kind (PIK)—a security paying interest or dividends in kind rather than in cash

Plan of reorganization—the terms under which a company expects to emerge from Chapter 11 bankruptcy

Portfolio cash flow—the cash flowing into a portfolio net of outflows

Portfolio insurance—a strategy involving the periodic sale of stock-index futures designed to eliminate downside risk in a portfolio at a minor up-front cost

Postpsetition interest—interest accruing from the date of a bankruptcy filing forward

Preferred stock—an equity security senior in priority to common stock with a specified entitlement to dividend payments

Prepackaged bankruptcy—a technique whereby each class of creditors in a bankruptcy agree on a plan of reorganization prior to the bankruptcy filing

Prepetition interest—interest accruing from the most recent coupon payment up to the date of a bankruptcy filing

Price/earnings (P/E) ratio—market price of a stock divided by the annualized earnings per share

Price-to-book-value ratio—market price of a stock divided by book value per share

Principal—the face amount or par value of a debt security

Principal-only mortgage security (PO)—principal payments stripped from a pool of mortgages which, in response to changes in interest rates, fluctuate in value in the same direction as conventional mortgages but with greater volatility

Private-market value—the price that a sophisticated businessperson would be likely to pay for a business based on the valuation multiples paid on similar transactions

Pro forma financial information—earnings and book value adjusted to reflect a recent or proposed merger, recapitalization, tender offer, or other extraordinary transaction

Proxy contest—a fight for corporate control through the solicitation of proxies or the election of directors

Prudent-man standard—the obligation under ERISA to restrict one's investments to those a "prudent" (conservative) person would make (see **Employee Retirement Income Security Act of 1974 (ERISA)**

Put option—a contract enabling the purchaser to sell a security at a fixed price on a particular date

Puttable bond—bond with embedded put features allowing holders to sell the bonds back to the issuer at a specified price and time (see **callable bond**)

Recapitalization—financial restructuring of a company whereby the company borrows against its assets and distributes the proceeds to shareholders

Relative-performance orientation—the tendency to evaluate investment results by comparing one's investment performance with that of the market as a whole

Return—potential gain

Rights offering—a financing technique whereby a company issues to its shareholders the preemptive right to purchase new stock (or bonds) in the company or occasionally in a subsidiary company

Risk—amount and probability of potential loss

Risk arbitrage—a specialized area involving investment in far-from-risk-free takeovers as well as spinoffs, liquidations, and other extraordinary corporate transactions

Secured debt—debt backed by a security interest in specific assets

Security—a marketable piece of paper representing the fractional ownership of a business or loan to a business or government entity

Self-tender—an offer by a company to repurchase its own securities

Senior-debt security—security with the highest priority in the hierarchy of a company's capital structure

Sensitivity analysis—a method of ascertaining the sensitivity of business value to small changes in the assumptions made by investors

Share buybacks—corporate stock repurchases

Shareholder's (owner's) equity—the residual after liabilities are subtracted from assets

Short-selling—the sale of a borrowed security (see **going long**)

Short-term relative-performance derby—manifestation of the tendency by institutional investors to measure investment results, not against an absolute standard, but against broad stock market indices resulting in an often speculative orientation

Sinking fund—obligation of a company to periodically retire part of a bond issue prior to maturity

Speculation—an asset having no underlying economics and throwing off no cash flow to the benefit of its owner (see **investment**)

Spinoff—the distribution of the shares of a subsidiary company to the shareholders of the parent company

Stock—a marketable piece of paper representing the fractional ownership of an underlying business

Stock index futures—contracts for the future delivery of a market basket of stocks

Stock market proxy—estimate of the price at which a company, or its subsidiaries considered separately, would trade in the stock market

Subordinated-debt security—security with a secondary priority in the hierarchy of a company's capital structure

Tactical-asset allocation—computer program designed to indicate whether stocks or bonds are a better buy

Takeover multiple—multiple of earnings, cash flow, or revenues paid to acquire a company

Tangible asset—an asset physically in existence

Tax-loss selling—selling just prior to year-end to realize losses for tax purposes

Technical analysis—analysis of past security-price fluctuations using charts

Tender offer—a cash bid to buy some or all of the securities of a target company

Thrift conversion—the conversion of a mutual thrift institution to stock ownership

Top-down investing—strategy involving making a macroeconomic forecast and then applying it to choose individual investments

Torpedo stocks—stocks for which investors have high expectations and which are therefore vulnerable to substantial price declines

Trader—a person whose job it is to buy and sell securities, earning a spread or commission for bringing buyers and sellers together

Trading flat—available for sale or purchase without payment for accrued interest

Treasury bills (T-bills)—non-interest-bearing obligations of the U.S. government, issued on a discount basis with original maturities ranging from three months to one year; the interest income from Treasury bills is the difference between the purchase price and par

Treasury bonds (T-bonds)—U.S. government obligations with original maturities of ten years or more; interest is paid semiannually

Treasury notes (T-notes)—U.S. government obligations with original maturities ranging from one to ten years; interest is paid semiannually

Value—the worth, calculated through fundamental analysis, of an asset, business, or security

Value investing—a risk-averse investment approach designed to buy securities at a discount from underlying value

Value investment—undervalued security; a bargain

Volume—the number of shares traded

Window dressing—the practice of making a portfolio look good for quarterly reporting purposes

Working capital—current assets minus current liabilities

Writing call options—selling call options on securities owned

Yield—return calculated over a specific period

Zero-coupon bond—a bond that accrues interest until maturity rather than paying it in cash

Bibliography

Bruck, Connie. *The Predators' Ball*. New York: Penguin, 1989.

Buffett, Warren E. "The Superinvestors of Graham-and-Doddsville." *Hermes* (Columbia Business School magazine) (Fall 1984) :4–15.

Ellis, Charles D., and James R. Vertin, eds. *Classics: An Investor's Anthology*. Homewood, Ill.: Dow Jones-Irwin, 1989.

Graham, Benjamin. *The Intelligent Investor*. 4th ed. New York: Harper & Row, 1973.

Graham, Benjamin, David L. Dodd, and Sidney Cottle. *Security Analysis*. New York: McGraw-Hill, 1962.

Lowenstein, Louis. *What's Wrong with Wall Street*. Reading, Mass.: Addison-Wesley, 1988.

Malkiel, Burton G. *A Random Walk down Wall Street*. 4th ed. New York: W. W. Norton, 1985.

Silber, John. *Straight Shooting: What's Wrong with America and How To Fix It*. New York: Harper & Row, 1989.

Soros, George. *The Alchemy of Finance*. New York: Simon & Schuster, 1987.

Index